W9-AGV-952

3 1230

Bulgakov, Mikhail
Afanas evich, 1891-
1940.

Notes on the cuff &
other stories.

DATE DUE		
APR 0 1 2008		
MAR 0 2013		

DISCARDED BY THE
URBANA FREE LIBRARY

URBANA FREE LIBRARY
(217-367-4057)

BAKER & TAYLOR BOOKS

Mikhail
BULGAKOV
Notes on the Cuff
& Other Stories

Translated by Alison Rice

Ardis

URBANA FREE LIBRARY

F

10-92 BT2750

Copyright © 1991 by Ardis Publishers
All rights reserved under International and
Pan-American Copyright Conventions
Printed in the United States of America

Ardis Publishers
2901 Heatherway
Ann Arbor, Michigan 48104

Book Design by Ross Teasley

Library of Congress Cataloging-in-Publication Data

Bulgakov, Mikhail Afanas'evich, 1891-1940.
[Short stories. English. Selections]

Notes on the cuff and other stories / Mikhail Bulgakov ;
translated by Alison Rice.
p.   cm.
Translated from the Russian.
ISBN 0-87501-057-1
1. Bulgakov, Mikhail Afanas'evich, 1891-1940—
Translations into English. I. Title.
PG3476.B78A27   1991
891.73'42--dc20   90-49545
CIP

CONTENTS

Introduction

The Mikhail Bulgakov who wrote *The Master and Margarita* seems a mysterious and powerful figure; the Bulgakov who is the author of the early works published here, however, is a more modest and accessible personality.

One of the pleasures of literary hindsight is discovering the source of later themes in early works and observing the initial personality of the writer in what is usually its least defended form. For example, one story in this collection, "The Red Crown," at first glance seems derivative of Chekhov's "Ward No. 7," but is actually very Bulgakovian in theme and autobiographical in detail. Here is the earliest example we have of Bulgakov's profound interest in the idea of the guilty bystander, how his conscience can become his punishment, and the form the expiation of this sin can take. The final statement of this material will be found, of course, in the characters of Pilate and the Master.

This is a very nervous collection of stories from the start of Bulgakov's career—a nervous man, writing in a nervous time. The cataclysm underlying all of the tension one can sense here is the harrowing experience of the Revolution and Civil War, as well as a brief exposure to World War I.

The first stories here are in large part autobiographical. Bulgakov, the son of a professor of theology at the Kiev Divinity Academy, came from a Russian family loyal to the monarchy. Since he was a doctor, he was mobilized by both the Ukrainian nationalist forces of Simon Petliura as well as the Whites during the many changes of power in Kiev, and was witness to atrocities committed by all sides. In 1919 he came down with typhus and was abandoned by the White Volunteer Army in the Caucasus as they evacuated, since travelling would have certainly killed him. It was at this point that he decided to quit medicine (to which he had been genuinely devoted), and become a writer (which had always been in the back of his mind). This was a remarkable decision, given the times he was living in. He was a twenty-eight-year-old with a wife, and he had fought on the wrong side—a fact which was becoming increasingly apparent as he recovered from the typhus. His state of mind and many of the externals of his life are well conveyed in "Notes on the Cuff" and "Bohemia." (However, literature is not life, and we may note that he left a few things out, such as the fact that his wife was actually with him most of the time, taking care of him when he was sick, and helping when he was well.)

What the reader will have difficulty in appreciating is the risk inherent in virtually all of Bulgakov's literary endeavors. He would always be criticized as an enemy of the Soviet regime—there is nothing new in that.

What is interesting, however, is that he truly *was* an enemy of the regime, yet he still managed to have a career. The "accursed feuilleton" which the narrator of "Notes on the Cuff" so regrets publishing has finally come to light, and it is a call to support the Volunteer Army of the Whites. Published in November 1919 in the town of Grozny, it shows both how convinced an anti-Bolshevik Bulgakov was—and how aware he was of the mistakes made by the White side. In it he contrasts the growing power of the Western countries which are now working for peace with the struggle of Russia to gain back its main cities. He foresees a dark future, however: "We shall have to pay, both literally and metaphorically. To pay for the insanity of March and October, for the Ukrainian separatist betrayers, for the way that the workers were debauched, for Brest . . . for everything!"

The stories translated here were published, for the most part, in periodicals widely read by the literary world, yet we find Bulgakov discussing his failed plans to emigrate and his dislike of rabidly Red critics ("Notes on the Cuff"). Part of this is due to what would later seem the relative freedom of this period in Russia, and part of it is due to the fact that one could still imagine that it was possible to be a member of the "loyal opposition." Bulgakov got further with this than most people of his background, to the point of becoming famous for his sympathetic portrayal of the enemy in the play *The Days of the Turbins,* but an outside observer may be excused for being stunned by Bulgakov's assumption that he had a right to exist in a world that was increasingly polarized along the lines of orthodox and ultra-orthodox.

The contradictory and colorful period of NEP (New Economic Policy) in the 1920s was in many respects ideal for Bulgakov as an observer of both politics and human nature. During NEP, economic freedoms were returned to some degree in hopes of reversing the catastrophic decline after the draconian regime of the first years after the Revolution. NEP spawned real economic improvement and a world of swindlers—not unlike the present period. The historic Russian distrust of men who make money came to the fore, and the press was filled with reports of amazingly creative schemes to cheat the government as well as the people. When Bulgakov uses the term "Nepman" in these stories, it is always negative, and in this he finds common ground with those Communist purists who were horrified to see what appeared to be the return, albeit briefly, of capitalism.

The various feuilletons here about the rebuilding of the Moscow infrastructure may strike the reader as somewhat odd, and there is a reason for this. The underlying assurances that Moscow is getting back to normal or even better than normal are addressed to a specific reading public, that of emigre Berlin. The paper *Nakanune (On the Eve)* was a particularly NEP-time enterprise. The paper was published in Berlin by

Russian emigres, subsidized by the Soviet government, and printed writers who lived in the Soviet
Union. But the paper wanted writers who had a certain profile: talented, cultured, supportive of the
Soviet Union but not usually of Communism. This
somewhat schizophrenic enterprise had as its aim the
calming of emigre fears about the Soviet Union and
the encouragement of those who were debating
whether to return to their native land. Bulgakov was
an ideal contributor: he, like *Nakanune*'s readers, had
no love for the regime, but a great sense of Moscow as
the center of Russian (as opposed to Soviet) culture.
So even as he describes the many things he does not
like in this new world, he made his Berlin readers long
to see some of the old landmarks, ballets, operas, and
theaters. But Bulgakov was eternally aesopian: a clever
reader would have understood that returning might
not really be such a good idea.

Ambivalence is present on almost every page as
well: this narrator is in love with this reborn city,
proud of it, proud to be a part of it, and proud to have
survived its worst years.

Bulgakov was dedicated to the country of Russian
literature, he had no use for the country of five-year-
plans, a fact which most of his works from this period
demonstrate, but he had the audacity, or perhaps the
naivete, to think that his talent was justification
enough for his survival, and that he would be allowed

to exist despite his stated dislike for virtually everything the proletarian control of literature endorsed.

The works published in *Nakanune* fall into two basic categories: artistic works—stories, and fragments of Bulgakov's longer works; and sketches of Moscow life during the twenties, pieces intended to inform the curious emigres about Moscow during NEP, as well as simply to record the vagaries of daily life during this era of great extremes.

The feuilleton as a genre came in with a vengeance during the early 1920s, good support for the theory that short forms prevail after a revolution. Humor was especially in demand: after the 1917 Revolutions there were dozens of humor journals and newspapers, and the publishing house Land and Factory put out numerous books in their famous series such as "The Happy Library," "Hippo" ("Begemot"), and "The Laugher." Hundreds of would-be feuilleton writers began busily unmasking evil everywhere (within the bounds of censorship), and the targets were not so very different from the ones which had attracted the famous pre-revolutionary satirists Sasha Chorny, Teffi, and others known as the "Satyriconians." They too had satirized bureaucracy, ignorance, the bourgeoisie, etc. The new label "Nepman" covered an old figure, but the critics of the twenties were watchful: there could be satire on the present, but it must always be with a smile, and it should not imply that human nature remained the same, i.e., sinful. If Communism could not change human nature, the critics and official guardians of the press did not want to know about it. From this point of view, Bulgakov's feuilletons were suspect, for too often they implied that the same prerevolutionary Russia could be found under a coat of red paint. But if the critics had not known who the author was, I do not think they would have noticed. Other more acceptable writers were quite as hard on contemporary foibles, but they did not have Bulgakov's defiant personal attitude. Bulgakov's characteristic interest in objects as well as people, and the comparisons are striking and fresh. The sensual world is evoked and enjoyed. The energy in these works is not just that of the young Soviet society, it is also that of the reporter newly come to the capital and still fascinated by it.

To provide a more comprehensive view of the city for his Berlin audience, Bulgakov would string together a series of scenes in his usual form of minichapters. In one of the best pieces of reportage, "The Capital in a Notebook," his subjects range from an embezzler who is sent to prison, to a doctor who makes his living as a furniture loader, practicing medicine only in his spare time, to a shocking schoolboy who is actually well-behaved.

This sketch is typical of many of the pieces on Moscow in the twenties. It displays Bulgakov's love of the city and his ironical attitude toward NEP, something common to most of the satirists working at this time. But the irony is offset by a cautious optimism, as if to say that despite all the bad things, everything is getting back to normal, and perhaps even a little better than normal.

The pertinence of these scenes of the city to Bulgakov's later work can be seen in the story "Forty Times Forty," published April 15, 1923. The panorama of Moscow seen from the top of the Nirenzee Building (where *Nakanune* had its offices) recalls Gogol's "Rome," and at the same time foreshadows the scenes of Moscow and Jerusalem which will play such an important role in *The Master and Margarita*.

A long piece on Kiev ("The City of Kiev," July 6, 1923) is a survey of contemporary Kiev and its problems. By turns ironic and melancholy, Bulgakov recalls the bad old days, remarking rather disingenuously that some day a new "contemporary Lev Tolstoi" will write an "amazing book" about the great battles of Kiev during the Civil War. Of course he has himself and his novel *The White Guard* in mind.

In addition to the works best characterized as reportage, Bulgakov wrote real feuilletons for *Nakanune*. One example is "The Komarov Case," an account of the trial of a mass murderer which focuses on the banality of this evil man.

But as much as Bulgakov is the bard of Moscow life, his best work of this period is about the process of becoming a writer. "Notes on the Cuff" is the first example of Bulgakov's favorite subject, the career of a writer and how the political world affects that career. The narrator of "Notes" is an artistic self-portrait, only the first of many; here he is, as usual, beleaguered, but, as usual, he is tremendously proud to be a Russian writer. The numerous complaints about the perils of existence for someone like himself in Civil War Russia is balanced by the clearly conveyed sense of the author's essential joy in his new profession.

"Notes on the Cuff" was the only important work Bulgakov managed to get published during his first year in Moscow. Part I appeared in *Nakanune's* literary supplement in June 1922. It was censored by the editors, who obviously thought the references to famine, typhus, and political clashes a little too sensitive for their readership. "Notes on the Cuff" is heavily autobiographical; this is not to say, however, that it gives a complete picture of Bulgakov's life during these years. Much is left out or abbreviated; it is a consciously literary work, in which every other line contains an allusion to Russian literature. While Bulgakov was fairly successful at getting his feuilletons into print (the present collection is only a small part of his output), his attempts to publish "Notes on the Cuff" met with constant frustration. After a two-year effort and only partial publication, the work was finally banned. Since the full text of the work has never been printed, we can only theorize about what else it may have included. The text of "Bohemia" shows marks of having once been part of the original "Notes on the Cuff," containing as it does characters with the same names, and a slightly different version of the writing of the collective play. More interesting, "Bohemia" fills in the various lacunae of "Notes," detailing why and how the hero goes to Tiflis, etc. The style and form—again with titled mini-chapters—also support the idea that this work was part of the original "Notes on the Cuff." Another story which is also probably connected to the censored first section of "Notes on the Cuff" is "The Unusual Adventures of a Doctor" which describes how the hero ended up in the Caucasus in the first place. This story is an early version of material which would later be used in the novel *The White Guard*. Bulgakov had a great reluctance to waste material, and it would be very like him to redo the censored sections as separate stories. If Bulgakov added a completely new section, as one of his references seems to suggest, it would probably have dealt with his work at *Gudok* and *Nakanune*—and would, in fact, be identical to the material included in the fragment "To a Secret Friend," written in 1929.

"Notes on the Cuff" is typical of Bulgakov's early prose in that it is thin on description and characterization, and pulses with a kind of nervous energy. The vitality and immediacy of the scenes here are created not through abundance of detail or analysis, but through Bulgakov's very selective arrangement of brief characteristic details and his wonderful ear for the spoken word, the language of the epoch sharp and precise as Morse code. Laconicism and fragmentation are marks of Bulgakov's early style, as is hemistich, a device to be expected from a playwright. Bulgakov fuses the comic and the pathetic in the same moment, and speaks directly to the reader's sympathies, creating a sense of intimacy with the reader, conveying the joy of becoming a writer, and the grief of having to do so during a time of disaster.

The style and structure of "Notes on the Cuff" mimic the lack of stability in Civil War Russia, as people's lives were disrupted in unpredictable ways. The disintegration of the stable world which normally serves as the artist's point of reference is what Mandelstam was referring to when he wrote that in the future the novel would be concerned with "the history of the disintegration of biography as a form of personal experience, even more than disintegration—the catastrophic destruction of biography." The phrase "destruction of biography" is a good description of what happened as writers were uprooted from their familiar worlds. Conscious that literature is a luxury in bad times, Bulgakov dedicated "Notes on the Cuff" to "the floating, travelling, and suffering writers of Russia."

The subject of this idiosyncratic work is literary apprenticeship, the obstacles to be overcome, the rewards and hopes of starting such a career. Bulgakov describes how he met a number of famous writers (virtually all the writers are real), and in this we may see a desire to associate with his professional colleagues, but the circumstances of these meetings were always fairly awful.

The problem of hunger, crucial for everyone, brings Knut Hamsun to the narrator's mind, but to seek a source for the style or content of this work in Hamsun seems to me a mistake. Hamsun's feverish style is not as compressed as Bulgakov's—a closer parallel to Bulgakov's staccato dialogue and elliptical descriptions can be found in Zamyatin. The theme of literary apprenticeship is reinforced by the lack of personal information; we have no sense that Bulgakov is married here, and the parts of his life not connected to literature are not described. Not that Bulgakov is always accurate in his portrayal of his literary career. The real Bulgakov had some success with his first plays in Vladikavkaz, but only the shameful collective play is mentioned in "Notes on the Cuff." In his literary autobiographies Bulgakov was never inclined to portray himself as successful.

Once the hero leaves the south, the style of "Notes" becomes calmer, reflecting a more stable life. The despairing wit of the exchanges between Bulgakov and Slyozkin is replaced by funny descriptions of the literary bureaucracy of LITO. This theme of office life turned diabolical would continue to appeal to Bulgakov throughout his career, and much of it starts with this first experience in the Moscow bureaucratic world. For instance, the incident of "losing" the LITO office (which had been moved without anyone telling him) was later used in the story "Diaboliad."

Throughout this work Bulgakov is writing with an eye to the future: "The literary historian should not forget," begins the section on LITO. Bulgakov, the doctor who became a writer later than he really wished to, never stopped meditating on what a writer's life means. At least five of his major works were about writers, and we can find a real sequel to "Notes on the Cuff" in *Theatrical Novel,* which continues the story of the same writer from his early days with the newspapers to his debut in the theater. In both works there is a great deal of bitter humor, as the novices stumble time after time, but they never regret their choice of profession. The difference between these two widely spaced works is interesting: the hero of "Notes on the Cuff" is capable of anger and resolute action, although he is often afraid. But in *Theatrical Novel,* Maxudov is a passive victim who ends up killing himself.

In "Notes on the Cuff" Bulgakov describes for the first time in his career the romance of becoming a writer. And it remained a romance, no matter how many unhappy experiences he and his heroes suffered.

Ellendea Proffer
Ann Arbor, 1991

Notes on the Cuff

I

The Caucasus[1]

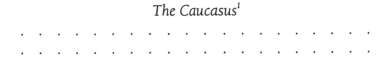

II

Recurrent Typhus

The contributor to the defunct *Russian Word*,[2] wearing gaiters and holding a cigar, grabbed the telegram from the table and with his practiced professional eye read it in a second from beginning to end.

His hand mechanically wrote in the margin "in two columns," but his lips unexpectedly pursed in a whistle, "Whew-ew!"

He was quiet for a moment. Then he abruptly tore off a piece of paper and jotted:

> *Forty miles to Tiflis it be...*
> *Who will sell a car to me?*

At the top: "Short Feuilleton," in the margin, "body," below, "The Rook."

1. This section is blank due to censorship reasons, although the device can sometimes be used for artistic effect, usually implying a romantic sort of *et cetera*. Since the final manuscript of this work did not survive, one can only assume that this section would have described Bulgakov's service in the White Army in the Caucasus.

2. *The Russian Word* was a famous Moscow newspaper (1895-1918) which published the best journalists of its time. For Bulgakov, it represented what journalism should be.

Suddenly he began to mutter like Dickens's Jingle: "I see. Uh-huh... I thought as much!... I may have to get going. So what! In Rome I have six thousand lire. *Credito Italiano*. What? Six... And actually I'm an Italian officer! Yes, indeed. *Finita la comedia!*"

And with another whistle, he pushed his cap to the back of his head and rushed out the door, with the telegram and feuilleton.

"Stop!" I yelled, coming to my senses, "Stop! What *Credito*? *Finita*?! What? A catastrophe?!"

But he was gone.

I wanted to rush out after him... but I suddenly just waved my hand, frowned listlessly and sat down on the small sofa. Wait a second, what's upsetting me? The incomprehensible *Credito*? The commotion? No, not that... Oh, yes. It's my head. It's been hurting for two days now. It bothers me. My head! And just now a strange chill ran down my spine. Then a second later, the opposite: my body is consumed by a dry heat, and my forehead feels unpleasant, damp. My temples are throbbing. I've caught a cold. This damned February fog! Just don't let me get sick... Just don't let me get sick!...

Everything seems strange, but then, after a month and a half I have become used to it. How wonderful, after the fog. Home. Cliffs and sea in a golden frame. Books in the bookcase. The rug on the divan is scratchy, there is no way to get comfortable, the pillow is hard, hard... But I won't get up for anything. How lazy! I don't want to so much as lift my arms. For half-an-hour now I have been thinking that I should reach out and take the powdered aspirin from the table, but I haven't done it...

"Mikhail, let me take your temperature!"

"Oh, I can't stand it!... There's nothing wrong with me..."

My God, my God, oh my God! A hundred and two... it can't possibly be typhus can it? Can it? It's not possible! Where from? But what if it is typhus?! Any other time, but not now! That would be terrible... It's nothing. Hypochondria. I just have a cold, that's all. It's influenza. I'll take some aspirin tonight and tomorrow I'll be as good as new!

A hundred and three point one!

"Doctor, it's not typhus is it? Not typhus? It's only the flu, isn't it? This fog..."

"Yes, yes... The fog. Take a deep breath, my dear fellow... Deeper... There!"

"Doctor, I have important business to take care of... It won't take long. Can I?"

"You must be crazy!..."

The cliffs, the sea, and the divan are red hot. You turn the pillow over, but as soon as you lay your head down, it's already hot. Never mind... I'll let tonight pass, but tomorrow I'll be up and about, up and about! And when that happens, I'll be on my way! I'll be on my way! There's no need to fall apart! Trifling influenza... It's good to be sick. To have a fever. To forget everything. Lie down for a while, take a rest, only, for heaven's sake, not now!... In this diabolical turmoil, I can't even do a little reading... But what I'd really like to do right now...

What would it be? Yes. Forests and mountains. Not these accursed Caucasian ones, though. But our distant ones... Melnikov-Pechersky.[3] A little, remote, snow-bound monastery. A small light glimmers and a bath is being heated... Those very forests and mountains. I would give half a kingdom to be in a hot steam bath right now, on a shelf. I would be well again in an instant... Then to throw myself naked into a snow-drift... Forests! Pine forests, dense forests... Ship timber. Pyotr in a green kaftan was chopping down the ship-timber forest. Hitherto... What a wonderful, decent, official word *hitherto* is! Forests, ravines, a carpet of pine needles, a white monastery. And a choir of nuns sings tenderly and sweetly:

To thee the champion leader a hymn of victory![4]...

3. Pavel Melnikov-Pechersky was a nineteenth-century novelist who wrote several works about the Old Believer colonies in the area between the Volga and the Urals. This paragraph contains Melnikov's main motifs.

4. A line from the acathistus hymn, "The Holy Virgin," yet another reference to the world of Melnikov's novels.

Oh, no! What nuns! There aren't any there! Where are the nuns, then? Black ones, white ones, thin ones, Vasnetsov ones?[5]...

"La-rissa Leontievna, where are the nu-uns?!"

"...He's delirious... delirious, poor thing!..."

"Nothing of the sort. And I'm not going to be delirious. Nuns! What, don't you remember? Well, give me the book. Over there, over there, on the third shelf. Melnikov-Pechersky..."

"Mikhail, you're not supposed to read!..."

"What? Why not? Tomorrow I'm going to get up! I'm going to see Petrov. You don't understand. They're going to abandon me! Abandon me!"

"Oh, all right, all right, get up! Here's the book."

A nice book. Even its smell is old, familiar. But the lines began to jump and jump, became crooked. I remembered. In the monastery they forged bank notes, Romanov bank notes. Oh dear, I used to have a memory! Not nuns, but notes...

My buns and boats![6]...

"Larissa Leontievna... Larochka! Do you like forests and mountains? I am going to join a monastery. Right now! To the backwoods, to a remote monastery. The

5. The narrator's incoherent state leads him to free association, from Melnikov's nuns and monks, to the Kiev church decorations done by the artist Vasnetsov.

6. This line and the previous reference to nuns and notes, come from a popular ditty of the time about changing bank notes, but the narrator changes the real word, buns, to nuns.

forest like a wall, a chorus of birdsong, no people...
I'm tired of this idiotic war! I'm going to run away to
Paris, write a novel there and then go to the
monastery. But tomorrow get Anna to wake me at
eight. You understand, I should have gone to see him
yesterday... Understand!"

"I understand, I understand, be quiet!"

Fog. Hot, reddish fog. Forests, forests... and water
quietly drips from a crevice onto a green stone. Such a
pure, twisting, crystal rivulet. Only you have to crawl
to it. But there you will drink your fill—and it vanishes as if by magic! Yet it is torture to crawl on the
pine needles, they are sticky and prickly. You open
your eyes, it isn't pine needles at all, but the sheets.

"Lord! What did you do to these sheets... Did you
pour sand on them, or what?... Wa-ter!"

"I'm coming, I'm coming!..."

"O-oh, they're hot, dreadful!"

"...terrible. It's a hundred and four point nine
again!"

"...an ice pack..."

"Doctor! I insist... Send me to Paris immediately! I
don't want to stay in Russia any longer... If you won't
send me, then be so kind as to hand me my Brow-...
Browning! Larochk-a-a! Get it for me!..."

"All right. All right. We'll get it for you. Don't upset
yourself!..."

———

Dusk. Dawn. Dusk... dawn. For the life of me, I can't remember...

My head! My head! There are no nuns or hymns of victory, but demons are blowing horns and tearing at my skull with red-hot hooks. My hea-ad!...

Dawn... dusk. Daw-... no, it's gone! Nothing is terrible, and nothing, nothing matters. My head doesn't ache. Dusk and a hundred and six ....

....

III

What Are We Going to Do?!

The novelist Yury Slyozkin sat in a plush armchair. In general, everything in the room was plush, making Yury seem somehow wildly dissonant. His head, bald from the typhus, was precisely that boyish head described by Mark Twain (an egg strewn with pepper). A service jacket, moth-eaten, with holes under the arms. On his legs gray puttees. One long, the other short. In his mouth a two-kopeck pipe. In his eyes fear and longing play leapfrog.

"What's go-ing to be-come of u-us now?" I asked and did not recognize my own voice. After the second attack, it was weak, thin and cracking.

"What? What?"

I turned over in bed and miserably looked out the window, where the still bare branches gently swayed. The exquisite sky, barely touched by the predawn glow, provided no answer, of course. Slyozkin was also silent, his disfigured head bowed.

A dress rustled in the next room. A female voice began to whisper:

"This evening the Ingush are going to plunder the city..."

Slyozkin twitched in his chair and corrected her, "Not the Ingush but the Ossetians. Not tonight, but tomorrow morning."

Perfume bottles responded nervously from the other side of the wall.

"My God! The Ossetians?! Then it's awful."

"Wha-at's the difference?..."

"What do you mean? But then, perhaps you aren't familiar with our customs. When the Ingush plunder... they plunder. But the Ossetians plunder and kill."

"Will they kill everyone?" Slyozkin asked matter-of-factly, puffing on his stinking pipe.

"Oh, my God! How strange you are! Not everyone... How can anyone say... But, what am I doing! I forgot. We're upsetting the patient."

A dress rustled. The hostess bent over me.

"I'm not up-set..."

"It's nothing!" Slyozkin cut in dryly. "Nothing!"

"What? Noth-ing?!"

"Yes, it's... The Ossetians and so on. Nonsense," he let out a puff of smoke.

My worn-out brain suddenly began to sing:

Mama! Mama! What are we going to do-o![7]

Slyozkin smirked with just the right side of his cheek. He thought for a moment. Then he had a sudden inspiration.

"We'll open a sub-department of the arts!"

"What's tha-at?"

"What?"

"What's a subapartment?"

"No! Sub-de-partment."

"Sub?"

"Uh-huh."

"Why sub?"

"Well, you see," he stirred, "there's the DNE[8] and the RNE.[9] D for department. Understand? And it in turn has a sub-department: sub. Understand?"

"Dee-any. Pe-ony. Barbusse. Barbos."

The hostess jumped up.

"For heaven's sake, don't talk to him! He'll start his raving again."

"Nonsense!" Yury said sternly. "Nonsense. And all of these Mingrelians, Imer-... What are they called? Circassians. They're just idiots."

---

7. A line from a popular song of the period.
8. Department of National Education.
9. Regional Department of National Education.

"Who-o?"

"They just run about. Shoot. At the moon. They won't plunder."

"But what'll hap-pen to us? Will we survive?"

"It's nothing. We'll open..."

"Of the arts?"

"Uh-huh. We'll have everything. Izo. Lito. Foto. Teo."[10]

"I don't under-stand."

"Mikhail, don't talk! Doctor..."

"I'll explain later. We'll have everything. I've already figured it out. What does it matter to us? We are apolitical. We are art."

"But how will we live?"

"We'll hide our money under a rug."

"What ru-..."

"Oh, that's what I did in that burg where I was in charge, the rug was on the wall. Whenever my wife and I got paid, we would hide the money behind the rug. It was alarming. But we ate. We ate well. Rations."

"But what about me?"

"You'll be chief of Lito. Yes."

"Of what?"

"Mikhail! I beg you!..."

10. Izo — Department of Fine Arts of the Commissariat of National Education; Lito — Literary Publishing Department of the People's Commissariat of National Education; Foto — Committee on Photography and Cinematography; Teo — Theatrical Department of the Board of Political Education.

IV

The Oil Lamp

The night swims. Resinous, black. No sleep. The oil lamp flickers. Outside, somewhere far off, there is shooting on the streets. My brain burns. It becomes hazy.

Mama! Mama! What are we going to do?!

Slyozkin is organizing over there. He is amassing them. Foto. Izo. Lito. Teo. Teo. Izo. Lizo. Tizo. He's piling up photograph boxes. What for? Lito. Literary men. We the wretched. Izo. Fizo. The Ingush, their eyes flashing, gallop up on horseback. They take the boxes away. Commotion. They are shooting at the moon. The doctor's aide pricks my feet with camphor. Third attack.

"O-oh! What's going to happen?! Let me go. I'm on my way, on my way, on my way."

"Be quiet, Mikhail dear, be quiet!"

After the morphine, the Ingush vanish. The velvety night gently flickers. The oil lamp glows like a divine eye and sings with a crystal voice:

"Ma-a-ma! Ma-a-ma!"

V

Here It Is — the Sub-Department

Sun! Behind the wheels of the carriages there are clouds of dust... In the echoing building people come and go... In a room on the fourth floor are two cupboards with their doors torn off, wobbly tables. Three young ladies with violet lips alternate between pounding loudly on typewriters and smoking.

Looking as if he were just down from the cross, a writer is sitting in the middle of it all and is creating the sub-department out of chaos. Teo. Izo. Pale blue actors' faces come at him. And demand money.

After the relapse came the doldrums. I am unsteady and nauseated. But I am in charge. Chief. Lito. I am getting used to it.

"Artdephead. The DNE. The editorial board."

Someone is walking between the tables. In a gray service jacket and monstrous riding-breeches. He thrusts his way into groups and they scatter. Like a torpedo boat cutting the water. Whoever he glances at turns pale. Eyes crawl under the table. Only the young ladies feel nothing! Young ladies are incapable of fear.

———

He approached. He gave me a piercing stare, extracted my soul, placed it in his palm and inspected it carefully. But the soul was crystal.

He put it back. He smiled benevolently.

"Lito chief?"

"Chief. Chief."

He went on his way. He looks like an okay guy. But there is no telling what he is doing here. He does not look like a Teo. Even less like a Lito.

A poetess arrived. Black beret. Her skirt was buttoned up the side and her stockings were sagging. She brought some poems.

> *La, la, la-la la-la*
> *In my heart beats a dynamo missile*
> *La, la, la-la.*

"Your little poems aren't bad. We'll... let's see... We'll read them at a recital."

The poetess's eyes lit up. She was a pretty nice girl. But why didn't she pull up her stockings?

VI

Gentleman of the Bed Chamber Pushkin

Everything was fine. Everything was wonderful.

And then everything fell apart because of Alexander Sergeevich Pushkin, may he rest in peace.

This is what happened:

The department of local poets made a nest for itself under the spiral staircase in the editorial office. Among these poets were a young guy in blue student pants, with a generator on his heart no less, a dense old man who began writing poetry in his sixties, and several other people.

The bold one with the aquiline face and huge revolver at his waist took an indirect approach. First he plunged his pen, which was brimming with ink, with all his might into the hearts of survivors from the old order who gad about from force of habit around the track to last summer's meet. Against the incessant roaring of the murky Terek River, he cursed the lilac and thundered:

> *You have heard enough of the moon*
> *and the seagull!*
> *I will praise the Cheka for you!!*

This was effective.

———

Next, someone else read a report on Gogol and Dostoevsky. And wiped them both from the face of the earth. He disparaged Pushkin, but only in passing. And promised a special report on him. On one June night, he lit into Pushkin. For wearing white pants,[11] for "I look ahead without fear,"[12] for "Gentleman-of-the-Bed-Chamberism and servile elements," and in general for "pseudorevolutionism and hypocrisy," for indecent poetry and running after women...

Sweating profusely in the oppressive heat, I sat in the first row and listened to the speaker tear Pushkin's white pants to pieces. However, when, after soothing his parched throat with a glass of water, he concluded with the suggestion that Pushkin be thrown on the ash heap, I smiled. I confess. I smiled enigmatically, the devil take me. Choose your smiles carefully!

"Step up and speak for the opposition."

"I don't want to."

"You have no civic courage."

"What's that? All right, I'll speak."

And I gave my speech so that the devil would take me. I had spent three days and three nights preparing it. I sat at an open window by a lamp with a red

11. His court dress.
12. A line from Pushkin's poem "Stanzas," celebrating the accession of Nicholas I.

shade. A book written by a man with burning eyes lay on my lap.

> *...false wisdom flickers and dims*
> *'Fore the eternal sun of the mind...*[13]

He said:

> *I accept the insult with indifference.*[14]

No, not with indifference! No I'll show them! I will. I shook my fist at the black night.

And I showed them. The department was thrown into confusion. The previous speaker was pinned to the mat. In the people's eyes, I read an unspoken, joyous, "Get him! Get him!"...
....
But in return, later!! Later...
I am a "wolf in sheep's clothing." I am a "Mr." I am a "bourgeois sympathizer"...

....
I am no longer chief of Lito. I am not chief of Teo.
I am a bastard cur in a garret. I sit making faces. They'll come to get me at night. I shudder.

13. A line from "Bacchic Song" by Pushkin.
14. A line from Pushkin's "Unto Myself I Reared a Monument."

....

Oh, dusty days. Oh, sultry nights.

————

In the summer of 1920 A.D., there was an apparition from Tiflis. A young man, all broken-down and worn out, with a wrinkled, old woman's face, arrived and introduced himself: a poet-brawler. He brought with him a small notebook which resembled a wine list. The small book contained his poems.

"Forget-me-not." Rhyme: "Stinking rot."

I'm going crazy, that's what...

The young man hated me at first glance. He's brawling on the pages of the newspaper (page 4, column 4). He writes about me. About Pushkin. And about nothing else. He hates Pushkin more than he does me. But what does that matter!

He is there and is to be found nowhere else.[15]

But I am done for, like a worm.

VII

The Bronze Collar

What an accursed city Tiflis is!

Another one has arrived! In a bronze collar. In a bro-onze one. This is how he made his appearance

15. A line from the prayer for the dead.

during the performance of the "living journal." I'm not joking!!

In a bronze one, understand! ....

....

The writer Slyozkin was sent to the devil. Despite his all-Russian fame and pregnant wife. And this one took his place. There's izo, plizo for you. There's money under the rug for you...

....

VIII

Baby in a Box

A halo of moonlight. Yury and I are sitting on the balcony and looking at the canopy of stars. But there is no relief. In a few hours the stars will fade and above us will blaze the fiery ball. And again, like beetles on pins, we will be wiped out.

A soft, continuous whine can be heard through the balcony door. In a godforsaken place, at the foot of the mountains in a strange city, in a toy-like, cage-like room, a son was born to the starving Slyozkin. They put him on the window in a box labeled: *Mme. Marie. Modes et robes.*

And he's whimpering in the box.

"Poor baby."

Not the baby. Us.

The mountains close in around us. Table Mountain sleeps in the moonlight. Far, far to the north are endless plains. To the south—ravines, abysses, turbulent rivers. Somewhere in the west is the sea. Over it shines the Golden Horn.[16]

....

...Have you seen a fly on flypaper?

When the whine quiets down, we go into the cage.

Tomatoes. A little black bread. And arrack. What foul vodka! Loathsome. But you have a drink—and things are better.

Then, when everyone around is sleeping soundly, the writer reads me his latest story. There is no one else to hear it.

The night swims. He finishes, and after carefully rolling up the manuscript, puts it under a pillow. There is no desk.

We talk in whispers until the pale dawn breaks.

What names on our shriveled tongues! What names! Pushkin's poems have a surprisingly soothing effect on our embittered souls. Russian writers, there is no need for bitterness!...

....

16. The Turkish port to which the Russian ships sailed.

Truth comes only through suffering. That is true, rest assured. But they do not pay money or hand out rations for the knowledge of truth. Sad, but true.

IX

A Passing Breeze

Evreinov[17] has arrived. In an ordinary white collar. From the Black Sea on his way to Petersburg. Somewhere in the north there used to be such a city.

Does it still exist? The writer laughs: he assures me that it does exist. But it takes a long time to get there: three years by freight car. The entire evening I stared at the white collar. The entire evening I listened to tales of adventure.

Fellow writers, in your lot...[18]

He sat there with no money. His things had been stolen...

...Again at Slyozkin's, on his last evening, Nikolai Nikolaevich sat at the piano, in the living room filled with cigarette smoke which the landlady had offered. With an iron staunchness, he endured the torture of the examination. Four poets, a poetess, and an artist

17. Nikolai Evreinov (1879-1953) was a brilliant playwright and director of experimental theater in St. Petersburg. He emigrated to France in 1920.

18. A line from Nekrasov's poem "In the Hospital," which continues: "There is something fateful."

(the department) sat sedately and drank him in with their eyes.

Evreinov is a resourceful person: "Here are *Musical Deviations...*"

And slowly turning toward the keys, he began. First of all... First of all, about how the elephant played the piano while visiting friends, then the piano-tuner in love, a dialogue between damask steel and gold and, finally, a polka.

After ten minutes, the department was put completely out of commission. It was no longer sitting, but was laid out on the floor side-by-side, waving its arms and groaning...

...The man with lively eyes left. No deviations!...

The breeze carried them along. Like leaves in the wind. One from Kerch to Vologda, another from Vologda to Kerch. One disheveled Osip[19] crawled in with a suitcase and said angrily, "I'm afraid we're not going to get there!"

Of course you're not going to get there if you don't know where you're going!

Yesterday Ryurik Ivnev[20] left. From Tiflis to Moscow.

19 This section, as commentators to the Moscow edition have pointed out, is structured on fragments and allusions to Russian literature of the nineteenth century. The lines about Kerch, etc., are from Ostrovsky's play *The Forest*; the Osip meant here is from Gogol's *Inspector General*. The effect is to connect the writers of the present with the writers of the past, and to once again reinforce the idea of continuity—even in a time of apparent discontinuity.

20. Ryurik Ivnev (1891-1981) was a poet and novelist, at first known as a Futurist.

"Things are better in Moscow."

He got so worn out travelling that one day he collapsed by a ditch.

"I'm not getting up! Something has to happen!"

It did: an acquaintance happened by the ditch—and fed him dinner.

Another poet. From Moscow to Tiflis.

"Things are better in Tiflis."

A third, Osip Mandelstam.[21] He walked in on an overcast day and held his head high, like a prince. His laconicism was devastating: "From the Crimea. Nasty. You buy manuscripts here?"

"...but we don't pay mon-..." I began but was unable to finish before he left. Who knows where...

The novelist Pilnyak.[22] To Rostov, by flour train, wearing a woman's blouse.

"Are things better in Rostov?"

"No, I'm only going to rest!!"

An eccentric—gold glasses.

Serafimovich[23]—from the north.

Tired eyes. Toneless voice. He gives a lecture to the department.

---

21. Osip Mandelstam (1891-1938) was one of Russia's greatest twentieth-century poets. Like Bulgakov, he was known for his wit.

22. Boris Pilnyak (1894-1937) was one of Russia's most famous writers after his novel *The Naked Year* was published in 1921.

23. Alexander Serafimovich (1863-1949) is best known as the author *The Iron Flood*.

"Remember, in Tolstoy there is a white handkerchief on a stick. First it hangs limp, then it flaps in the breeze again. It's like a living being—the handkerchief... He wrote some sort of warning label for the vodka bottle against drunkenness. He wrote a phrase. He crossed out a word and wrote another above it. He thought for a minute and then crossed it out again. And this happened several times. However, the phrase came out perfectly turned. The way they write now... it's incredible! You take it. You read it through once. No! You don't understand. Again, the same thing. So you put it aside..."

The local department sits pressed against the wall *in corpore*. They look as though they don't understand this. That's their business!

Serafimovich left... Intermission.

X

The Story of the Great Writers

The subdepartment set designer drew Anton Pavlovich Chekhov with a crooked nose and wearing such a monstrous pince-nez that from a distance it looked as though Chekhov was wearing automobile goggles.

We placed him on a large easel. The set contained a reddish pavilion, a small table with a decanter and small lamp.

I read the introductory article, "On Chekhov's Humor." But either because I had not eaten for three days, or maybe for some other reason, my brain was somewhat clouded. The theater was packed. Now and then I fumbled. I saw hundreds of indistinct faces, piled up to the cupola. And if only someone had smiled. The applause, nevertheless, was friendly. I thought in confusion: that's for whatever just ended. With relief I departed to the wings. I earned my two thousand, let someone else be the fall guy now.

Passing through the smoking room, I heard a Red Army man complain, "I wish they would get blown to bits with their humor! You come to the Caucasus and they fool with your head!..."

He's absolutely right, this Tula soldier. I hid in my favorite place, a dark corner behind the props. And I listened to the clamor of voices coming from the auditorium. Hurrah! They are laughing. Well done, actors. "Surgery" came to the rescue and the story about how the bureaucrat sneezed.

A hit! Success! Slyozkin rushed into my rat hole and sputtered, rubbing his hands, "Write another program!"

After the "Evening of Chekhov's Humor," we decided to put on a "Pushkin Evening."

Yury and I lovingly drew up a program.

"This blockhead doesn't know how to draw," raged Slyozkin, "let's have Marya Ivanovna do it!"

At that instant I had an ominous premonition... In my opinion, this Marya Ivanovna knows how to draw like I know how to play the violin... I decided this as soon as she appeared in the Subdepartment and announced that she had been a pupil of "N" himself. (She was immediately appointed chief of Izo.) But since I know nothing about art, I kept quiet.

Exactly half an hour before the curtain, I walked into the set-designer's room and froze... Nozdrev[24] himself looked out at me from a gold frame. He looked just great. Bugged, impudent eyes and even with one of his side-whiskers thinner than the other. The illusion was so great that it seemed as though he were about to burst out in a chuckle and say, "I, friend, have come from the fair. Congratulate me, I gambled away all my money!"

I don't know how I must have looked, but the artist was mortally offended. She blushed profusely under a layer of powder and narrowed her eyes.

"You, apparently... uh... don't like it?"

"No. What do you mean. Heh-heh! It's very... nice. Very nice. Only there... the side-whisker..."

"What?... The side-whisker? Well, you must never have seen Pushkin! Congratulations! And a writer at

---

24. A character in Gogol's *Dead Souls*.

that! Ha-ha! Do you think I should have drawn Pushkin clean-shaven?!"

"I'm sorry, side-whiskers are side-whiskers, but Pushkin didn't play cards, and even if he did, he wouldn't have cheated!"

"What cards? I don't understand! I see you are making fun of me!"

"You are the one who's making fun. Your Pushkin has the eyes of a rogue!"

"A-ah... so tha-at's it!"

She threw down the brush. From the door: "I'm going to complain to the Subdepartment about you!"

What happened next! What happened next!... As soon as the curtains opened and Nozdrev, smirking insolently, appeared before the darkened auditorium, the first laughter rippled. God! The audience had decided that after Chekhov's humor there was going to be Pushkin's humor! Soaked in cold sweat, I began talking about "the northern lights on the snowy wastes of Russian literature..." People giggled in the auditorium about the side-whiskers, Nozdrev stuck up behind my back and seemed to mutter to me, "If I were your boss, I'd hang you on the nearest tree!"

So I was unable to restrain myself and giggled. The success was shattering, phenomenal. Neither before nor since have I heard such thunderous applause directed at me. But later there was a *crescendo*... During the play, when Salieri poisoned Mozart, the theater expressed its satisfaction with an approving laugh and loud shouts of "Encore!!"

I scurried out of the theater like a rat, and dimly saw the poet-brawler rushing to the editorial office with a notebook...

I just knew it!... On the kiosk was a newspaper and on the fourth page was:

PUSHKIN AGAIN!

For Christ's sake! Why can't this brawler die! Everyone else here has typhus, after all. Why can't he get sick? This cretin is going to get me arrested!...

Oh, the devil's own toy doll, Izo!

It's over. Everything's over!... The evenings have been banned...

...The awful autumn is coming. Driving rain lashes down. I have no idea—what we are going to eat? What are we going to eat?!...

XI

A Foot-Cloth and a Black Mouse

....

Hungry, late in the evening, I walk among the puddles in the darkness. Everything is boarded up. On my feet are ragged socks and worn-out boots. There is no sky. In its place hangs a huge foot-cloth. I am drunk with despair. And I mutter, "Alexander Pushkin. *Lumen coeli. Sancta Rosa.* And his threat is like thunder."[25]

Am I going crazy?! A shadow flees from the street-light. I know, it's my shadow. But it is wearing a top hat. I am wearing a visored cap. To keep from starving, I took my top hat to the bazaar. Some kind people bought it...

Despair. Above my head a foot-cloth and a black mouse is gnawing at my heart...

XII

Almost Like in Knut Hamsun[26]

I starve..

....

....

XIII

Escape, Escape!

One hundred thousand... I have one hundred thousand!...

I earned it!

25. A line from Pushkin's poem, "There lived a poor knight."
26. Knut Hamsun (1859-1952) is the famed Norwegian novelist who wrote *Hunger,* suitably enough, about a starving writer.

An assistant attorney, a local, taught me. He came to me as I sat silently with my head in my hands and said: "I don't have any money either. There is only one solution, we have to write a play. About local life. A revolutionary one. We'll sell it..."

I stared at him blankly and responded: "I can't write anything about local life, revolutionary or counter-revolutionary. I don't know the customs. I can't write anything at all. I'm tired, and it seems I have no literary talent."

He answered: "You're talking nonsense. It's just because you're hungry. Be a man. Customs, that's nothing! I know the customs like the back of my hand. We'll write it together. We'll split the money fifty-fifty."

That very evening we began writing. He had a hot, potbellied stove. His wife hung up washing on a string in the room and then gave us some salad with vegetable oil and tea with saccharin. He supplied typical names for the characters, told me about the customs, and I worked on the plot. He did, too. And his wife sat down and gave us advice. At that moment I was convinced that both of them had much more literary talent than I. But I felt no envy, because I promised myself that this would be the last play I would ever write...

So we wrote.

He leaned against the stove and said, "I love to create!"

I scratched away with a pen...

Seven days later the three-act play was finished. When I read it over to myself, in my unheated room at night, I am not ashamed to admit that I burst into tears! As far as talentlessness went, it was truly phenomenal, shattering. Something stupid and insolent peered out from each line of this collective creation. I could not believe my eyes! I was crazy—what could I hope for, if I wrote like that?! Shame looked out at me from the damp, green walls and the terrifying black windows. I started to tear up the manuscript. But I stopped myself. For suddenly, with extraordinary, remarkable clarity, I realized that those who say never destroy what has been written are right! You can tear it up, burn it... hide it from others. But from yourself—never! It is finished! It is indelible. I wrote this amazing thing. It is finished!...

The play created a furor in the local subdepartment. It was immediately bought for two hundred thousand. And two weeks later it went on.

Daggers, gas lights, and eyes gleamed in the mist of a thousand breaths. After the heroic horsemen rushed in during the third act and grabbed the police-officer and guards, Chechens, Kabardians, and Ingush cried, "Hah! Scoundrel! That's what he deserves!"

And following the lead of the subdepartment's young ladies, they called out: "Author!"

There were handshakes in the wings.

"Vanderful play!"
And we were invited to the aul[27]...

...Escape! Escape! With a hundred thousand I can leave here. Onward. To the sea. Over a sea, and a sea and France—dry land—to Paris!

...Driving rain cut my face and, shivering in a raincoat, I ran through the alleys for the last time—homeward...

...You novelists and playwrights in Paris, in Berlin, try it. Try, just for the sake of it, to write something worse! Even if you are as talented as Kuprin, Bunin, or Gorky, you won't be able to. I have broken the record! For a collective creation. Three of us wrote it: me, an assistant attorney, and starvation. At the beginning of 1921...

XIV

....

The city at the foot of the mountains disappeared. To hell with it ....

Tsikhidziri. Makhindzhauri. Cape Green! The magnolias are in bloom. White flowers the size of plates. Bananas. Palms! I swear, I saw it with my own eyes, a

27. A native village in the Caucasus.

palm tree growing right out of the ground. And the sea constantly sings by the granite cliff. What the books say is no lie: the sun sinks into the sea. Maritime splendor. A gorgeous vista. A sheer cliff, covered with vines. Chakva. Tsikhidziri. Cape Green.

Where am I going? Where? I am wearing my last shirt. Crooked letters are on my cuffs. And painful hieroglyphs are in my heart. I have been able to decipher only one of those mysterious signs. It means: woe is me. Who is going to interpret the rest for me?

I lie as though dead on the pebbles smoothed by the salt water. Hunger has left me without an ounce of strength. My head aches from early morning until late at night. And here is the night, by the sea. I cannot see it, I only hear it drone. Waves roll in and roll out. And a late wave whispers. Then suddenly from behind the dark cape come three tiers of lights.

The *Polatsky* is sailing to the Golden Horn.

....

Tears are as salty as sea water.

————————

I saw an unknown poet. He was walking around the bazaar and trying to sell the hat on his head. The Georgians laughed at him.

He smiled in embarrassment and explained that he was not joking. He was selling his hat because his money had been stolen. He lied. His money had gone long ago. And he had not eaten for three days. Later, after we had shared a pound of churek,[28] he admitted the truth. He told me that he was travelling from Penza to Yalta. I almost burst out laughing. But suddenly I remembered: what am I doing myself?

The cup is filled to overflowing. At twelve o'clock the "new chief" arrived.

He came out and announced: "We have to try something else. We don't need this parnographia anymore: *Woe from Wit* and *The Inspector General*. Gogols. Mogols. We're going to write out our own plays."

Then he got into his car and drove away.

His face is imprinted on my brain forever.

An hour later I sold my overcoat at the bazaar. In the evening a steamship was leaving. It would not let me on. Understand? Would not let me on...

All right! Let the Golden Horn shine. I'll never get there. I have only so much energy. It's all gone. I'm starving, I'm broken! There's no blood left in my brain.

28. Unleavened bread made in the Caucasus.

I'm weak and afraid. But I can't stay here any longer. In which case, I should...

XV

Homeward

Home. By the sea. Then in a freight car. Not enough money, so then on foot.

But home. My life is ruined. Home.

To Moscow! To Moscow!!

....

Farewell Tsikhidziri. Farewell Makhindzhauri. Cape Green!

XVI

The Moscow Abyss. Tavlam.

Fathomless darkness. Clank. Crash. The wheels turn again, but now quieter, quieter. And they stop. The end. The true end of all ends. My final destination. This is Moscow. M - o - s - c - o - w.

For a second my attention is caught by a drawn-out, forceful sound which comes out of the darkness. In my head is an eerie thunder:

C'est la lu-u-tte fina-a-le!...
...L'internationa-a-a-le!!

And here, just as hoarse and terrifying, "With the Internationale!!"

In the darkness a row of freight cars. The student car falls silent...

I finally decide to jump down. Some soft body slipped out from under me with a groan. Then I caught hold of the rails and fell into some place even lower. God, is there really an abyss under my feet?...

Gray bodies, bearing monstrous loads on their shoulders, began to flow past... flow past...

A female voice, "Oh... I can't!"

In the black fog I saw a medical student. Writhing in pain, she had traveled beside me for three days.

"Let me take it."

In an instant, the black abyss seemed to stagger and turn green. "How much have you got here?"

"A hundred pounds... The flour has been pounded down."

Amid sparks, we lurched and zigzagged toward the lights.

Rays radiate from them. The queer gray snake winds its way across them. A glass cupola. A long, drawn-out rumble. A blinding light in the eyes. Ticket. Wicket gate. A snatch of voices. Foul language grates on the ear. Again darkness. Again rays of light. Darkness. Moscow! Moscow.

The cart was stacked as high as the cupolas of churches, as high as the stars mounted on velvet. With a clatter, it rolled, and the demonic voices of gray overalls cursed the stuck cart and the man clucking to the horse. A herd followed behind the cart. And the long, whitish overcoat of the student could be seen first to the right, then to the left. But finally the wheels found their way out of the confusion, and bearded faces stopped flashing past. We rode along the torn-up pavement. Darkness was everywhere. Where are we? What place is this? It doesn't matter. It makes no difference. All of Moscow is black, black, black. The houses are silent. They look on, dry and cold. O-ho-ho. A church swims by. Its appearance is blurred, dismayed. It vanishes into the darkness.

Two o'clock in the morning. Where shall I spend the night? Houses and more houses! What could be easier?... I could knock at any of them. Would you let me spend the night? Certainly not!

The voice of the medical student: "Where are you going?"

"I don't know."

"What do you mean...?"

There are kind souls in the world. You see, the apartment manager's room is next door. He still hasn't returned from the country. She said I could spend the night...

"Oh, thank you very much. Tomorrow I will locate my friends." My spirits lifted a little. It is a strange thing, as soon as you find out you will have a roof over your head at night, you suddenly feel the effects of not having slept for three days.

On the bridge, two lights break up the gloom. From the bridge we plop into the darkness again. Then a streetlight. A gray fence. On it is a poster. Huge bright letters. A word. Good gracious! What sort of word is that? Tavlam. What does it mean? What is it supposed to mean?

The Twelfth Anniversary of Vladimir Mayakovsky.

The cart stopped. They took the things off. I sat down on the curb and, spellbound, stared at the word. Oh, it is a good word. And I, a wretched provincial, snickered in the mountains at the Artdephead! Ah, the devil take it. Oh, Moscow is not as bad as they say. I had the agonizing desire to introduce myself to the hero of the day. I have never seen him, but I know... I know. He is about forty, very short, bald, wears glasses,[29] very animated. Very short, rolled-up trousers. He is employed. Doesn't smoke. He has a large apartment with portieres, which he shares with an attorney who is no longer an attorney but the superintendent of a government building. He lives in an office with a cold fireplace. He loves butter, funny poems, and a tidy room. His favorite author is Conan Doyle. His fa-

29. All this is ironic—the famous Futurist poet Mayakovsky was tall, did not wear glasses, etc.

vorite opera, *Eugene Onegin*. He makes meat balls for himself on a Primus stove. He hopes that sooner or later the attorney-superintendent, whom he cannot stand, will move out, and he'll get married, and will live gloriously in the five rooms.

The cart screeched, shuddered, continued on its way, and stopped again. Neither storm nor tempest has overthrown that immortal citizen, Ivan Ivanich Ivanov. Near a building, which in the darkness looked, due to fear, as though it had about fifteen stories, the cart grew noticeably thinner. In the inky gloom a figure darted from it toward the entryway and whispered, "Papa, have you got the butter?... Papa, have you got the shortening?... Papa, have you got the white flour?"

Papa stood in the darkness and muttered, "Shortening... yeah; butter... yeah; white and dark... yeah."

Then there was a flash in the infernal darkness as papa's short finger counted out twenty notes for the cart driver.

There will be more storms. Oh, big storms will come! And everyone can die. But this papa will not die!

———————

The cart became a huge platform on which the medical student's bundle and my travelling bag seemed lost. We sat down, our legs dangling, and rode away into the dark depths.

XVII

Building No. 4, 6th Entryway,
3rd Floor, Apt. 50, Room 7

As a matter of fact, I do not know why I crossed the whole of Moscow and came to this particular colossal building. The piece of paper I carefully carried with me from the mountain kingdom could have had a connection with all the six-story buildings, but more likely has nothing to do with any one of them.

In the sixth entryway I'm standing by the cage-like shaft of the lifeless elevator. I caught my breath. A door. Two signs. "Apt. 50." The other was mysterious, "Art."[30] I have to catch my breath. Whatever might happen, my fate was being decided.

I knocked at the unlocked door. In the semi-dark entrance hall there was a huge box of paper and the top of a piano. I glimpsed a smoky room full of women. Someone began to pound on a typewriter. It stopped. Someone said in a bass voice, "Meyerhold."[31]

"Where is Lito?" I asked, leaning my elbows on the wooden counter.

---

30. In Russian, the abbreviation for "artistic literature" can be read as "badly."
31. The famed Russian avant-garde theater director.

The woman at the counter shrugged her shoulders in irritation. She did not know. A second also did not know. But here is a darkish corridor. It's dim, guess work.

I opened one door, the bathroom. But there's a small scrap of paper on another door. It's tacked on crooked and an edge is folded up. Li. Ah! Thank God. Yes, Lito. Again my heart. Muffled voices could be heard from behind the door: du-du-du...

I closed my eyes for a second and imagined. Beyond the door. There is—the following: in the first room a huge rug, a writing desk, and bookshelves. A solemn silence. At the desk is a secretary, probably one of the names I knew from the magazines. More doors. The chief's office. Even greater, deeper silence. Shelves. In an armchair, of course... who? Lito? In Moscow? Yes, Maxim Gorky! *The Lower Depths*. *Mother*. Who else would it be? Du-du-du... They are talking... And what if it's Bryusov talking with Bely?[32]...

I knocked lightly at the door. The du-du-du stopped, then a muffled, "Yes." Then the du-du-du again. I pulled on the handle, and it came off in my hand. I froze, a great beginning to one's career—I've broken it! I knocked again. "Yes! Yes!"

"I can't get in!" I shouted.

A voice could be heard through the keyhole, "Turn the handle to the right, then to the left, you have locked us in..."

---

32. Bryusov and Bely were major writers of the Symbolist period.

To the right, to the left, the door gently gave way, and...

XVIII

After Gorky, I'm Number One

I'm in the wrong place! Lito? A dacha wicker chair. A bare wooden table. An open cupboard. A small table upside down in the corner. And two people. One tall, very young, wearing a pince-nez. What struck me were his puttees. They were white, and he was holding a cracked briefcase and a small sack... The other, a graying old man with lively, almost laughing eyes, was wearing a papakha[33] and soldier's greatcoat. It was full of holes and the pockets hung in shreds. His puttees were gray and he wore patent leather dress shoes with bows.

With a lifeless look, I examined his face, then the walls, looking for more doors. But there were no doors. The room, with its wiring torn out, led nowhere. *Tout.* Somewhat tongue-tied: "Is this... Lito?"

"Yes."

"Would it be possible to see the chief?"

The old man answered gently, "That's me."

---

33. A tall Caucasian hat usually made of sheepskin.

Then he picked up a huge page from the Moscow newspaper that lay on the table, tore off a quarter of it, sprinkled some *makhorka*[34] on it, rolled a cigarette and asked me, "Do you have a match?"

I mechanically struck a match, and then under the gentle, inquiring gaze of the old man took the cherished piece of paper out of my pocket.

The old man bent over it, while I anxiously wondered who he could be... He most resembled a shaved Emile Zola.

The young guy, leaning over the old man's shoulder, also read it. They finished and looked at me with something like both confusion and respect.

The old man: "So you...?"

I answered: "I would like a position in Lito."

The young one exclaimed excitedly: "Wonderful!... You know..."

He grabbed the old man by the arm and began to whisper: "Du-du-du."

The old man spun on his heels and grabbed a pen from the table. And the young one said in a rush: "Write a statement."

My statement was in my breast pocket. I gave it to him.

The old man waved the pen. It went: krak! and jumped, tearing the paper. He stuck it into the ink well. But it was dry.

"Don't we have a pencil?"

34. Cheap tobacco.

I took out a pencil and the chief wrote in a slanting hand "I request that this person be appointed Lito's secretary. Signature."

Open-mouthed, I looked at the dashing flourish for a few seconds.

The young man turned me around by the sleeve, "Go upstairs, quickly, before he leaves. Quickly."

I flew like an arrow upstairs. I tore through the door, sweeping through the room with the women, and went into the office. The person sitting in the office took my piece of paper and wrote: App. sec. A letter. A hook. He yawned and said, "Go downstairs."

In a daze I flew downstairs again. A typewriter flashed by. Not a bass, but a silvery soprano said: "Meyerhold. Theatrical October..."

The young man bustled around the old one and chuckled, "He appointed you? Wonderful! We'll manage it! We'll manage everything!"

At this point he slapped me on the shoulder, "Don't lose heart! Everything will work out!"

I have not been able to stand familiarity from childhood, and from childhood I have been its victim. But at this point, I was feeling so overwhelmed by everything that had happened that I could just manage to say weakly, "But tables... chairs... ink..."

The young man shouted in excitement, "We'll get them! Excellent! We'll get everything!"

And turning to the old man, he winked in my direction: "A practical guy! The way he immediately thought of tables! He'll sort everything out for us!"

Appointed secretary. Lord! Lito. In Moscow. Maxim Gorky...
The Lower Depths... Scheherazade... *Mother*.

The young man shook the sack, spread a newspaper out on the table and poured about five pounds of peas onto it.
"There you go. A quarter of your rations."

XIX

I Get Lito Going

The literary historian should not forget:
At the end of the 1921, there were three people in the Republic who dealt with literature: an old man (dramas; he did not, of course, turn out to be Emile Zola, but someone I had never heard of), a young man (the old man's assistant, also someone I had never heard of—poetry) and me (who had not written a thing).

For the historian: Lito had no chairs, no tables, no ink, no lamps, no books, no writers, no readers. In short: there was nothing.

And I. Yes, out of the void I managed to obtain a mahogany writing desk, an antique. In it I found an old, yellowed, gold-trimmed pasteboard with the words: "...women in low-cut ball gowns. Soldiers in frock coats with epaulets; civilians in tail coats and ribbons. Students in uniforms. Moscow in 1899."

There was a tender, sweet smell. The drawer had once contained a bottle of expensive French perfume. After the desk, a chair appeared. Then ink and paper and, finally, a young lady, slow-moving and sad.

On my instructions, she placed everything that was in the cupboard in piles on the table: brochures on some kind of "saboteurs," twelve issues of a St. Petersburg newspaper and a stack of green and red tickets for a governors' department congress. And suddenly it began to look like an office. The old man and the young man were ecstatic. They clapped me tenderly on the shoulder and disappeared somewhere.

The sad young lady and I sat there together for hours on end. I at the desk and she at the table. I read *The Three Musketeers* by the inimitable Dumas, which I found on the floor in the bathroom, and the young lady sat silently and from time to time produced a deep and weary sigh.

"What are you crying about?" I asked.

In reply she began to sob and wring her hands. Then she said: "I have discovered that the man I married is a gangster."

I doubted there was anything in this world that could surprise me after these past two years. But... I stared blankly at the young lady...

"Don't cry. It happens."

And I asked her to tell me about it.

Wiping away her tears with a handkerchief, she told me that she had married a student, had an enlargement of his picture made and hung it in the living room. A police agent came, looked at the photo and said that it was not Karasev at all, but Dolsky, alias Gluzman, alias Senka Moment.

"Mo-ment," said the poor young lady, and she shuddered and dried her face.

So he took to his heels? Good riddance.

————————

However, three days passed. Nothing. No one came. Nothing at all. The young lady and I...

A thought came to me today: Lito has not been started. There is life above us. The tramping of feet. There is also something happening on the other side of the wall. Sometimes the hollow clatter of typewriters, sometimes laughter. Some clean-shaven people come there. Meyerhold is phenomenally popular in this building, but he has yet to appear.

Nothing is happening with us, however. No paper. Nothing. I decided to get Lito going.

A woman with a bundle of newspapers was climbing the stairs. On top in red pencil were the words: for Izo.

"What about Lito?"

She looked at me in fright and did not answer. I went upstairs. I went up to a young lady who was sitting beneath the sign: secretary.

After listening to me, she looked in fright at her neighbor.

"Well, Lito it's true..." said the first.

The second replied: "There is paper for them, Lidochka."

"Why haven't you sent it?" I asked icily.

They looked at me tensely: "We didn't think you were there."

————

Lito has been started. A second lot of paper arrived today from the young ladies upstairs. A woman wearing a shawl brought it. With a book: sign, please.

I wrote a note to the supply department: give me a typewriter. Two days later the man arrived and shrugged his shoulders: "Do you really need a typewriter?"

"I think more than anyone else in this building does."

The old man turned up. The young one also. When the old man saw a typewriter, and when I said that he needed to sign the papers, he looked at me fixedly for a long time and chewed his lips: "You have something. You should try and get us academician rations."

The gangster's wife and I began filling out a payroll form. Lito caught on to the general movement.

To my future biographer: I'm the one who did this.

XX

The First Swallows

At 11 o'clock in the morning, a young, apparently very cold, poet arrived. He said quietly: "Shtorn."

"What can I do for you?"

"I would like a job with Lito."

I unrolled a sheet of paper with the heading, "Staff." Lito is supposed to have eighteen employees. I anxiously cherished ideas of these assignments:

Instructors for the poetry department:

Bryusov, Bely... etc.

Prose-writers:

Gorky, Veresaev, Shmelyov, Zaitsev, Serafimovich[35]... etc.

But none of those listed ever appeared.

---

35. All major older writers.

In a bold hand I wrote on Shtorn's application: req. appt'd. instr. Acting dir. A letter. A hook.

"Go upstairs, before he leaves."

Then the curly, ruddy, and very jovial poet Skartsev arrived.

"Go upstairs, before he leaves."

A remarkably gloomy person wearing glasses, about twenty-five years old, so compactly sculpted that he appeared to be cast of brass, arrived from Siberia.

"Go upstairs..."

But he answered, "I'm not going anywhere."

He sat down in the corner on a broken, wobbly chair, took out a piece of paper and began writing something with short strokes. He had obviously been around.

The door opened, and someone in a good warm overcoat and sealskin hat came in. He turned out to be a poet. Sasha.

The old man wrote the magic words. Sasha attentively surveyed the room, thoughtfully touched the dangling, bare wire and for some reason glanced at the cupboard. He sighed.

He sat down next to me, and said confidentially: "Will there be any money?..."

XXI

We Are Building Up Steam

There was no space at the tables. Everyone was writing slogans, including yet another newcomer, a lively and noisy character in gold-rimmed glasses who called himself the king of reporters. The king appeared at a quarter to nine the morning after we had received an advance and said: "Listen, I hear you've been given some money."

He went to work for us.

The story behind the slogans was as follows.

A note arrived from upstairs: Lito is urgently requested to present a number of slogans by 12 o'clock on such and such a day.

In theory, such an assignment should have been carried out as follows: the old man, in my presence, should have issued the hue and cry wherever it was assumed there might be writers. Slogans should have poured in from every direction, telegraphed, written, and spoken. Then a commission should have selected the best from the thousands of slogans and presented them by 12 o'clock on such and such a day. Then I and the office under my management (i.e., the sad gangster's wife) should have filled out a requisition, received money, and paid the most deserving for the best slogans.

But that's theory.

In practice, however:

1) No call could be sent out, because there was no one to send it to. At that time all the writers were in view: all those I've listed plus the king.

2) Number one being impossible, there consequently could be no deluge of slogans.

3) The slogans could not be presented by 12 o'clock on such and such a day because the note requesting them arrived at 1:26 p.m. on that same day.

4) The requisition could not be filled out, since there was no column "for slogans." But—

The old man had a small sum: for travel.

Therefore:

a) Everyone present is to write slogans as quickly as possible.

b) To ensure complete impartiality, the commission for reviewing the slogans will also be composed of all those present.

c) After the best slogans are selected, fifteen thousand rubles will be paid for each.

We sat down at 1:50 p.m. and the slogans were ready at 3:00 p.m. We each managed to produce 5-6 slogans, with the exception of the king who wrote 19 in both verse and prose.

The commission was exacting and impartial.

I, author of slogans, had no connection to the I who critiqued and accepted the slogans.

As a result, the following were accepted:

From the old man—three slogans.
From the young man—three slogans, etc., etc.
In short, each person received 45 thousand.

————

Ooh-ooh, what a wind... There it goes, it is beginning to drizzle. A meat pie on Trubnoi Street, wet from the rain, but maddeningly delicious. A small tube of saccharin. Two pounds of white bread.

I caught up with Shtorn. He was also chewing on something.

XXII

An Unexpected Nightmare

...I swear, it's a dream!! What kind of wizardry is this?!

Today I was two hours late for work.

I turned the handle, opened the door, walked in and looked: the room was empty. But so empty! Not only were there no tables, sad woman, or typewriters... there were not even any electric wires. Nothing.

So, it was a dream... Of course... of course...

For a long time now it has seemed that everything around me is a mirage. A shimmering mirage. There, where yesterday... Although, what the devil, why yesterday?! A hundred years ago... in eternity... perhaps, it never was... perhaps it is not now? Kanatchikov's dacha!...[36]

So, the kind old man... the young one... sad Shtorn... the typewriter... slogans... never existed?

They existed. I am not crazy. They existed, the devil take it!!

Well, where's it all gone to?

With an unsteady gait, my lids lowered to hide the look in my eyes (so I would not immediately be seized and thrown out), I walked along the semi-dark corridor. Finally I became convinced that something was wrong. In the darkness above the door leading into the adjoining, brightly lit room, there burned a fiery sign, like at the cinema:

1836

ON MARCH 25 AN EXTREMELY UNUSUAL THING HAPPENED IN ST. PETERSBURG. THE BARBER IVAN YAKOVLEVICH...[37]

I did not read any further but slipped away in terror. At the counter I stopped, lowered my eyes even more and asked hoarsely:

"Did you see where Lito went?"

36. Lunatic asylum in the Moscow suburbs.
37. The opening lines of Gogol's story, "The Nose."

An irritated, gloomy woman with a crimson ribbon in her dark hair answered, "What Lito... I don't know."

I closed my eyes. Another female voice said sympathetically, "It's not here at all. You've come to the wrong place. It's on Volkhonka Street."

I immediately went cold. I went out into the courtyard. Wiped the sweat from my brow. Decided to walk back across the whole of Moscow to Razumikhin's. Forget everything. For if I am quiet, keep silent, no one will ever find out. I will live on the floor at Razumikhin's. He will not turn me out—a mentally ill person.

———

However, in my heart I still harbored a last, faint hope. So I went. I went. This six-story building was indeed strange. The whole thing was shot through with longitudinal passageways, like an ant-hill, so that it was possible to walk through the entire place from end to end without coming out into the street. I walked along warm convolutions and from time to time came across niches of some kind behind wooden partitions. Reddish, uneconomical bulbs burned. I encountered worried people who were hurrying somewhere. Dozens of women were sitting around. Typewriters clattered. Signs flashed by. Financial department. National minority. Coming across brightly lit landings, I again walked into darkness. Finally, I came out into a landing, and stared fixedly around. Here was some other realm... Stupid. The further I went, the slimmer my chances of finding the bewitched Lito. Hopeless. I went downstairs and out into the street. I looked around, it proved to be the first entryway.

An evil gust of wind. The sky began to pour cold streams again. I pulled my summer cap further down on my head and raised the collar of my overcoat. Several minutes later, through the large slits in their soles, my boots filled with water. It was a relief. I did not entertain the thought of managing to arrive home dry. I did not jump from cobblestone to cobblestone, lengthening my journey, but walked straight through the puddles.

XXIII

2nd Entryway, 1st Floor, Apt. 23, Rm. 40

A fiery sign:
ABSOLUTE NONSENSE GOES ON IN THE WORLD. SOMETIMES THE COMPLETELY IMPROBABLE HAPPENS: SUDDENLY THAT VERY NOSE WHICH TRAVELED ABOUT WITH THE RANK OF A CIVIL SERVANT AND CAUSED SUCH A RUCKUS IN THE CITY, FOUND ITSELF, AS THOUGH NOTHING HAD HAPPENED, BACK WHERE IT BELONGED AGAIN...[38]

38. Ending of "The Nose."

———

Morning brings wisdom. That is the honest truth. When the cold awakened me in the morning and I sat on the divan, hair tousled, things seemed a little clearer in my head.

Logically: did it really exist? Well, of course it existed. After all, I can remember both the date and my name. They must have moved it... Well, that just means I have to find it. Now, what did that woman sitting next to her say? On Volkhonka... Oh, nonsense! They could steal anything they wanted from under those women's noses. On the whole, I don't know why they are kept on, those women. An Egyptian torture.

After dressing and drinking some water, which I had saved from yesterday in a glass, I ate a piece of bread and a mashed potato and made a plan.

Six entryways times six floors = 36. Thirty-six times two apartments = 72. Seventy-two times six rooms = 432 rooms. Is it possible to find it? Possible. Yesterday I searched two or three horizontals unsystematically. Today I will systematically cover the whole building both vertically and horizontally. And I will find it. Only, of course, if it did not jump into the fourth dimension. If it has, then, yes. The end.

———

At the second entryway, I came face to face with— Shtorn!

Good God! A blood brother...

It turned out that yesterday, an hour before I arrived, the head of the administration department appeared with two workers and transferred Lito to the second entryway, first floor, apartment 23, room 40.

The Musical Department had taken our place.

"Why?"

"I don't know. But why didn't you come yesterday? The old man was worried."

"For goodness sake! How was I supposed to know where you had gone? You should have left a note on the door."

"Well, we thought someone would tell you..."

I gritted my teeth, "Have you seen those women? The ones next to us..."

Shtorn said, "That's true."

XXIV

Full Steam

...After I got a room, I felt rejuvenated. At our Lito office, they screwed in a bulb. I got a ribbon for the typewriter. Then another young lady arrived. Req. appt. clerk.

Manuscripts began to arrive from the provinces. Then yet another wonderful young lady. A journalist. A fine, good-humored comrade. Req. appt. secretary of the bureau for artistic feuilletons.

Finally, a young man from the south. A journalist. By his name was written the last "Req." There were no more jobs. Lito was full. There was an outpouring of work.

XXV

Money! Money!

Twelve tablets of saccharin and nothing else...
...My sheets or my jacket?...[39]
There is not so much as a hint of payment.
...Today I went upstairs. The women received me very coldly. For some reason they found Lito intolerable.
"I would like to check our requisition."
"What for?"
"I want to see if everything has been entered."
"Go see Madame Kritskaya."
Madame Kritskaya stood up, shook her bun of graying hair and said, going pale, "It's been lost."
Pause.
"And you said nothing?"
Madame Kritskaya answered tearfully, "Oh, my head is reeling. What can I do, it's beyond human understanding. I wrote the requisition seven times, they returned it. It's not correct. You won't get paid anyway. You hired someone without permission."

39. Meaning, which to sell.

———

The devil take them all! Nekrasov and the resurrected alcoholics. I rushed out. Corridors again. Darkness. Light. Light. Darkness. Meyerhold. Personnel. The lights burn during the day. A gray overcoat. A woman in wet felt boots. Tables.

"Who's been hired without permission?!"

Reply, "No one."

But the best of all: Lito's founder, the old man, wasn't! What? And I wasn't either?! What on earth?!

"You probably didn't fill in the form, did you?"

"I didn't? I filled in four forms for you. And personally placed them in your hands. Along with those I wrote previously, that makes a total of 113 forms."

"Well, it's gotten lost. Fill in another one."

———

Three days passed in this way. Three days later everything had been straightened out. New requisitions had been written.

I am opposed to the death sentence. But if Madame Kritskaya is taken to be shot, I will go along to watch. The same for the young lady in the sealskin hat. And Lidochka, the clerk's assistant.

"...Take them away! A clean sweep!"

Madame Kritskaya was left with the requisitions in her hand, and I solemnly announced: she won't send them on. I cannot understand why this devilish hair bun is here. What idiot hired her? In this case, it's definitely Fate.

———

A week passed. I was on the fifth floor, in the fourth entryway. They had begun printing there. Another form was needed, but I could not find the chairman of the tax-accounting commission anywhere the next day.

I sold my sheets.

———

There will not be any money for two weeks.

———

Rumor has it that everyone in the building is going to be paid a 500 ruble advance.

———

The rumor is true. Everyone sat down and wrote requisitions. For four days.

I went with my requisitions for my advance. I obtained everything. Everything was stamped before my eyes. However, I got so furious that, running from the second to the fifth floor, I bent an iron bolt that was sticking out of the wall in the corridor.

I handed in my requisitions. They will be sent to some other building at the other end of Moscow... There they were approved. Returned. Then the money...

———

Today I received money. Money!

Ten minutes before going to the cash register, the woman on the first floor, who was supposed to give the final stamp, said: "It's not done properly. You will have to keep the requisition."

I don't remember exactly what happened. A fog.

It seems I painfully cried out something like, "Are you making fun of me?"

The woman opened her mouth, "A-ah, you are so..."

Then I calmed down. I calmed down. I said that I was upset. I apologized. I took back what I had said. She agreed to correct it with red ink. She jotted: Issued. A flourish.

To the cash register. Magical words: the cash register. I could not believe it even when the cashier took out the notes.

Then I came to my senses: money!

———

From the time I began writing the requisition to the time I received the money from the cash register, twenty-two days and three hours had elapsed.

My apartment's cleaned out. No jackets. No sheets. No books.

XXVI

How One Should Eat

I got sick. Carelessness. Today I ate some red borscht with meat. Small goldish disks floated in it (fat). Three bowls. Three pounds of white bread in one day. I ate slightly salted pickles. When I had eaten my fill, I made some tea. I drank four glasses with sugar. I wanted to sleep. I lay down on the divan and fell asleep...

I had a dream that I was Lev Tolstoy at Yasnaya Polyana. And I am married to Sophie Andreevna.[40] I am sitting upstairs in my study. I am supposed to be writing. But I do not know what to write. And people keep coming in and saying: "Please eat."

I am afraid to leave. And like a fool I feel that there is a great misunderstanding here. You see, I did not write *War and Peace*. But nevertheless here I sit. And

40. Tolstoy's wife.

Sophie Andreevna herself comes up the wooden staircase and says, "Come. Vegetarian meal."

Suddenly I become angry.

"What? Vegetarianism? Send for meat! Make meatballs. A shot of vodka."

She bursts into tears and some Dukhobor[41] with a broad, thick red beard rushes in and says reproachfully, "Vodka? Oh, dear! What do you mean, Lev Ivanovich?"

"What do you mean by calling me Lev Ivanovich? It's Nikolaevich! Get out of my house! Out! I don't want any Dukhobors here."

There was some kind of uproar.

I woke up extremely ill and down. Dusk. Somewhere on the other side of the wall someone was playing a harmonica.

I went to the mirror. There was that face. Red beard, white cheekbones, red eyelids. But that's nothing, just look at the eyes. Not good. Again that glitter.

———

Advice: avoid this glitter. As soon as it appears, take out a loan from a bourgeois (no repayment), buy groceries and eat. But do not eat your fill right away. On the first day, bouillon and a little white bread. Gradually, gradually.

41. A member of a religious sect which rejects the rites of the Russian Orthodox Church. They usually had beards and long hair and wore baggy pants and long, knee-length shirts tied at the waist with twine.

I did not like my dream either. It was a nasty dream.

I drank some more tea. I thought back over the past week. On Monday, I ate potatoes with vegetable oil and a quarter pound of bread. I drank two glasses of tea with saccharin. I did not eat anything on Tuesday, but drank five glasses of tea. On Wednesday, I borrowed two pounds of bread from the locksmith. I drank tea, but I had run out of saccharin. On Thursday, I ate magnificently. At two o'clock I went to see an acquaintance. A maid in a white apron opened the door.

A strange feeling. As though it were ten years ago. At three o'clock I hear the maid beginning to set the table in the dining room. We sit and talk (I shaved this morning). They curse the bolsheviks and say how exhausted they are. I realize they are waiting for me to leave. But I do not leave.

Finally the hostess says, "Perhaps you'd like to eat with us? Or perhaps not?"

"Thank you. It would be my pleasure."

We ate: a macaroni soup and white bread, meat patties with cucumbers for the main course, then rice kasha with jam, and tea with jam.

I have a repulsive confession to make. When I left, I imagined their house being searched. They come. Dig up everything. Find gold coins in underpants in the closet. In the pantry flour and ham. They take the host...

It is abominable to think this way, but that is what I thought.

You, who sit starving in a garret over a feuilleton, do not follow the example of the overfastidious Knut Hamsun. Go to those who live in seven rooms, and eat. On Friday, I ate soup and a potato patty at the cafeteria, and today, Saturday, I got some money, over-ate, and got sick.

XXVII

A Thunderstorm. Snow.

Something threatening begins to hang in the air. I have already developed a sixth sense. Something is beginning to tremble beneath our Lito.

The old man appeared today and said, jabbing his finger at the ceiling above which the young ladies were concealed, "There is a plot against me."

As soon as I heard this, I immediately calculated how many saccharin tablets I had left... Enough for five to six days.

———

The old man burst boisterously into the room.

"I've put an end to their plot," he said. No sooner had he spoken than the head of an old crone in a shawl poked through the door and growled, "Who is here? Sign."

I signed.

On the paper was written: As of such and such a date, Lito is liquidated.

...Like the captain of a ship, I was the last to leave. There was business: I ordered the district Lito to collect and file away the works of Nekrasov and the Reformed Alcoholic, the Famine collections[42] as well as the poems and instructions. I switched the light off with my own hand and left. Snow immediately fell from the sky. Then rain. Then neither snow nor rain, but something which came from all sides and clung to my face.

During days of cutbacks in staff and such weather, Moscow is awful. It was in fact a cutback in staff. In other apartments of that terrible building, other people were also being laid off.

But: Madame Kritskaya, Lidochka, and the sealskin hat remained.

1920-21

---

42. These are in-jokes: the works of the nineteenth-century poet Nekrasov had just been reissued for his centenary celebration, the "Famine" collections were actually collections being prepared by Lito at the time, and the play "The Reformed Alcoholic" had actually been submitted by one Grigorovsky.

Bohemia

I

How to Survive with the Aid of Literature.
Astride a Play to Tiflis.

If someone asked me what I deserve, I would say in all honesty before God that I deserve hard labor.

Not because of Tiflis, however; I did not do anything wrong in Tiflis. Because of Vladikavkaz.

I was living out my last days in Vladikavkaz, and the terrible specter of hunger, (Cliché! Cliché!... "terrible specter"... However, I don't give a damn! These memoirs will never be published!) as I was saying, the terrible specter of hunger knocked at the door of my modest apartment which I had obtained with a permit. And right after the specter knocked Attorney Genzulaev, a pure soul with a brush mustache and an inspired face.

We talked, and here I include a stenographic record:

"What are you so down in the mouth about?" (Genzulaev)

"Apparently, I'm doomed to die of starvation in this crummy Vladikavkaz of yours..."

"There's no question about that. Vladikavkaz is a crummy city. I doubt there's a crummier city anywhere in the world. But why do you have to starve to death?"

"There's nothing else I can do. I've exhausted all possibilities. The Subdepartment of the Arts has no money, so they can't pay any salaries. I won't be making any more introductory speeches before plays.[1] I had a feuilleton printed in the local Vladikavkaz newspaper for which I received 1,250 rubles and a promise that they would turn me over to the special department[2] if another one like it ever appeared in print."

"Why?" (Genzulaev was alarmed. Understandably. If they wanted to turn me over to the special department, I must be suspect.)

"For my mocking tone."

"Oh, rubbish. They just don't understand anything about feuilletons here. I'll tell you what..."

And here is what Genzulaev did. He incited me to write a revolutionary play with him about native life. I'm slandering Genzulaev here. He pushed me and, because of my youth and inexperience, I agreed. What does Genzulaev know about the writing of plays? Nothing whatsoever, it was plain to see. Right away he openly admits that he sincerely detests literature, and I myself hated literature, you better believe, even more than he did. But Genzulaev knows native life like the back of his hand, if, of course, you can call native life a combination of shishkebab houses, breakfasts against

1. See the events in *Notes on the Cuff*.
2. Secret police.

a backdrop of the most repulsive mountains in the world, daggers of inferior steel, sinewy horses, taverns, and disgusting music that wrenches the soul.

Therefore, I will write the play and Genzulaev will add the local color.

"Only idiots would buy this play."

"We're the idiots if we don't manage to sell this play."

We wrote it in seven-and-a-half days, thus spending half a day more than was necessary to create the world. Despite this, it turned out even worse than the world.

I can say one thing: if there is ever a competition to see who can write the most stupid, untalented, and presumptuous play, ours will receive first prize (however, several plays from 1921-26 now come to mind, and I begin to have my doubts...), well, if not first prize, certainly second or third.

In short, after writing this play I am forever stigmatized, and naturally I can only hope that the play will molder in the bowels of the local Subdepartment of the Arts. As for the receipt, the devil take it, it can stay there. It was two hundred thousand rubles. One hundred for me. One hundred for Genzulaev. The play ran for three nights (a record), and the authors were called on stage. Genzulaev came out and took a bow, laying his hand against his clavicle. Then I came out and made faces for a long time so that I would be unrecognizable in the photograph (which was taken from below with magnesium). Due to these faces, a rumor spread throughout the town that I was brilliant but mad. It was annoying, especially because the faces were totally unnecessary, since the photographer who took our picture was requisitioned and assigned to the theater, so nothing came out on the photograph but a shotgun, the inscription, "Glory to..." and a blurred streak.

I ate up seven thousand in two days and decided to use the remaining ninety-three to leave Vladikavkaz.

———

Why? Why Tiflis of all places? For the life of me, I do not now recall. However, I remember I was told that:

1) in Tiflis all the stores are open,
2) in Tiflis there is wine,
3) in Tiflis it is very hot and the fruit is cheap,
4) in Tiflis there are many newspapers, etc., etc.

I decided to go. First, I packed my things. I took all my worldly possessions: a blanket, some underclothes, and a Primus stove.

In 1921 things were not quite the same as in 1924. To be more precise, it was impossible to just pack up and go wherever you wanted! Apparently, those who were in charge of civilian travel reasoned something like this:

"If everyone started traveling, then where would we be?"

Therefore, a permit was required. I immediately submitted an application to the appropriate authorities, and where it asked, "What is the purpose of your trip?" I wrote with pride, "I am going to Tiflis for the production of my revolutionary play."

In all of Vladikavkaz there was only one person who did not know me by sight, and it happened to be the gallant young fellow with the pistol on his hip who stood as if nailed to the spot by the table where permits for travel to Tiflis were issued.

When my turn came to receive a permit and I reached out to take it, the young man started to give it to me, but then stopped and said in an authoritative, high-pitched voice, "What is the purpose of your trip?"

"The production of my revolutionary play."

Then the young man sealed the permit in an envelope and handed both me and the envelope over to someone with a rifle, saying, "Take him to the special department."

"What for?"

The young man did not answer.

A very bright sun (the only good thing in Vladikavkaz) beamed down on me as I walked along the road with the man carrying the rifle to my left. He decided to strike up a conversation with me and said, "We're going to be passing through the bazaar now, but don't even think about escaping. Nothing good will come of it."

"Even if you begged me to do it, I wouldn't," I replied in all honesty.

Then I offered him a cigarette.

Smoking companionably, we arrived at the special department. As we crossed the courtyard, I fleetingly recalled all my crimes. There were three.

1) In 1907 I was given one ruble and 50 kopecks to buy Kraevich's *Physics* but spent it at the cinema.

2) In 1913 I got married against the wishes of my mother.

3) In 1921 I wrote that celebrated feuilleton.

The play? But that play could hardly be called criminal, could it? Quite the contrary.

For the information of those who have never been inside the special department, it is a large room with a rug on the floor, a huge desk of unbelievable proportions, eight telephones of different designs with green, orange, and gray cords attached, and behind the desk, a small man in military uniform with a very pleasant face.

The luxuriant crowns of the chestnut trees could be seen through the open windows. Upon seeing me, the man sitting at the desk attempted to change the pleasant expression on his face to an unfriendly and unpleasant one, but was only partially successful.

He took a photograph out of the desk drawer and began scrutinizing both it and me in turn.

"Oh, no. That's not me," I hurriedly announced.

"You could have shaved off the mustache," Mr. Pleasant responded thoughtfully.

"Yes, but if you look closely," I said, "the guy in the picture has hair the color of black shoe polish and is about forty-five. I am blond and twenty-eight."

"Dye?" the small man asked with uncertainty.

"But what about the bald spot? And besides look closely at the nose. I beg you to take a good look at the nose."

The small man peered at my nose. He was overcome with despair.

"I believe you. There's no resemblance."

There was a pause, and a ray of sunlight sprang up in the inkwell.

"Are you an accountant?"

"God forbid."

Pause. The crowns of the chestnuts. The stucco ceiling. Cupids.

"What is the purpose of your trip to Tiflis? Answer immediately without thinking," the small man said in a rush.

"To stage my revolutionary play," I answered in a rush.

The small man opened his mouth, but recoiled and was completely radiated by the sun.

"You write plays?"

"Yes, I have to."

"No kidding. Was the play you wrote a good one?"

There was something in his voice that would have touched any heart but mine. I repeat, I deserve hard labor. Looking away, I said:

"Yes, a good one."

Yes. Yes. Yes. This was my fourth crime, the worst one of all. If I had wanted to remain pure before the special department, I should have answered: "No. It's not a good play. It's junk. I just really want to go to Tiflis."

I looked at the toes of my worn-out boots and did not speak. I came to myself when the small man handed me a cigarette and my travel permit.

He said to the guy with the rifle, "Show the writer to the door."

The special department! I must forget about it! You see, now I have confessed. I have shed the guilt I have carried for three years. What I committed in the special department was, for me, worse than sabotage, counter-revolution or abuse of power.

But I must forget it!!!

II

Eternal Wanderers

People say that in 1924 it was easy to travel from Vladikavkaz to Tiflis; you simply hire a car in Vladikavkaz and drive along the remarkably scenic Georgian

Military Highway. It is only two hundred and ten versts.[3] However, in Vladikavkaz in 1921 the very word, "hire," sounded like a word from a foreign language.

In order to travel you had to go with your blanket and Primus stove to the station and then walk along the tracks, peering into the innumerable freight cars. Wiping the sweat from my brow, on track seven I saw a man with a fan-shaped beard standing in slippers by an open freight car. He was rinsing out a kettle and repeating the vile word, "Baku."

"Take me with you," I requested.

"No," replied the man with the beard.

"Please, so I can stage my revolutionary play," I said.

"No."

The bearded man carried the kettle up a plank and into the freight car. I sat on my blanket beside the hot rails and lit a cigarette. A stifling, intense heat filled the spaces between the freight cars, and I quenched my thirst at the faucet by the tracks. Then I sat down again and felt the scorching heat radiated by the freight car. The bearded man stuck his head out.

"What's your play about?" he asked.

"Here."

I unrolled my blanket and took out my play.

"You wrote it yourself?" the proprietor of the freight car asked dubiously.

"With Genzulaev."

"Never heard of him."

3. A Russian unit of distance, in this case equal to about 6.5 miles.

"I really need to leave."

"Well, I'm expecting two more, but if they don't show up, perhaps I'll take you. Only don't have any designs on the plank bed. Don't think that just because you wrote a play you can try anything funny. It's a long journey, and as a matter of fact, we ourselves are from the Political Education Committee."

"I won't try anything funny," I said, feeling a breath of hope in the searing heat. "I can sleep on the floor."

———

Sitting down on the plank bed, the beard said, "Don't you have any food?"

"I have a little money."

The bearded man thought for a moment.

"I'll tell you what... you can share our food on the journey. But you'll have to help with our railway newspaper. Can you write something for our paper?"

"Anything you want," I assured him as I took possession of my ration and bit into the upper crust.

"Even feuilletons?" he asked, and the look on his face made it obvious that he thought me a liar.

"Feuilletons are my specialty."

Three faces appeared out of the shadows of the plank bed, along with bare feet. They all looked at me.

"Fyodor! There's room for one more on the plank bed. That son-of-a-bitch Stepanov isn't coming," the feet said in a bass voice. "I'll make room for Comrade Feuilletonist."

"Okay, make room for him," bearded Fyodor said in confusion. "What feuilleton are you going to write?"

"The Eternal Wanderers."

"How will it begin?" asked a voice from the plank bed. "Come over here and have some tea with us."

"Sounds good—Eternal Wanderers," responded Fyodor, taking off his boots. "You should have said you wrote feuilletons to start with, instead of sitting on the tracks for two hours. Welcome aboard."

———

A vast and wondrous evening replaces the scorching day in Vladikavkaz. The evening's edge is the bluish mountains. They are shrouded in evening mist. The plain forms the bottom of the cup. And along the bottom, jolting slightly, wheels began to turn. Eternal Wanderers. Farewell forever, Genzulaev! Farewell, Vladikavkaz!

1925

The Red Crown
Historia Morbi

Most of all I hate the sun, loud human voices, and pounding. Rapid, rapid pounding. I am so afraid of people that if I hear someone else's footsteps and the sound of voices in the corridor in the evening, I start to scream. Because of this I have a special room, the quietest and the best, No. 27, at the very end of the corridor. No one can get to me. But in order to protect myself further, I kept begging Ivan Vasilievich for a long time (actually, I cried in front of him), to give me an official typed authorization. He consented and wrote that I was under his protection and that no one had the right to take me away. But, to tell you the truth, I did not have much confidence in the weight of his signature. So he persuaded a professor to sign it too, and affixed a round blue seal to the paper. That made all the difference. I know of many instances where people have avoided death solely because they had a piece of paper with a round blue seal on it in their pockets. True, that worker in Berdyansk with the cheek smeared with soot was hung from a lamppost after they found a crumpled piece of paper with a stamp on it in his boot. But that was altogether different. He was a criminal Bolshevik and the blue seal was a criminal seal. It reserved him a place on that lamppost and the lamppost was the reason for my illness (don't worry, I know perfectly well that I am ill).

In fact, something had happened to me even before Kolya. I walked away in order to avoid seeing a man being hanged, but fear walked with me in my trembling legs. At the time, of course, there was nothing I could do, but now I would boldly say, "General, you are an animal! How dare you hang people!"

This alone shows you that I'm no coward. I did not go on about the seal because I am afraid of death. Oh, no. I am not afraid of that. I am going to shoot myself, and it will be soon, because Kolya will drive me to despair. I will shoot myself so that I do not have to see or hear Kolya. As for the thought that other people might come... It is loathsome.

———

For days on end I have been lying on the couch and staring out the window. Above our green garden is an empty void. Beyond it the yellow bulk of a seven-story building turns its deaf, windowless wall to me, and right under the roof is a rusty square. A sign. *Dental Laboratory.* In white letters. At first I hated it. Then I got used to it and if it were gone I might even miss it. It can be seen clearly the whole day. I focus my attention on it and ponder many important things. But evening is falling. The cupola darkens, the white letters fade from view. I become gray and dissolve in the gloom just like my thoughts. Twilight. A frightening and portentous time of day. Everything fades, everything becomes indistinct. A pale ginger cat begins to slink along the corridor with velvety steps and from time to time I scream. But I will not allow a lamp to be lit because the glare of the lamp will cause me to wring my hands and sob all night. It is better to wait submissively for the moment when that most important last picture begins to burn in the quivering darkness.

———

My aged mother said to me: "I can't go on like this much longer. All I see is madness. You are the oldest, and I know that you love him. Bring Kolya back. Bring him back. You are the oldest."

I said nothing.

So she put all of her yearning and all of her pain into her words.

"Find him. You pretend that nothing can be done. But I know you. You are intelligent, you have long understood that this is all madness. Bring him to me for a day. For just one day. I'll let him go again."

She was lying. Would she really let him go again?

I said nothing.

"I only want to kiss his eyes. I know he will be killed. Don't you understand? He's my baby. Who else can I ask? You are the oldest. Bring him."

I could not stand it, so avoiding her eyes, I said, "Okay."

But she grabbed my sleeve and turned me around so that she could look into my face.

"No, you will swear that you will bring him back alive."

How could I swear any such thing?

But being the insane person that I am, I did it: "I swear."

————

My mother is fainthearted. With that thought I left. But in Berdyansk I saw the crooked lamppost. General, Sir, I agree that I was no less criminal than you, I accept great responsibility for the man smeared with soot, but my brother does not have anything to do with it. He is nineteen years old.

After Berdyansk, I resolutely fulfilled my oath and found him by a small stream twenty versts away. The day was unusually bright. Along the road to the village, from which came the smell of ashes, a cavalry column moved slowly, stirring up clouds of white dust. He rode at the end of the first rank, with the visor of his cap pulled down over his eyes. I remember every detail. The right spur came all the way down to his heel. The strap of his cap stretched across his cheek and down under his chin.

"Kolya. Kolya!" I yelled, and ran down to the roadside ditch.

He started. Along the ranks the sullen, sweaty soldiers turned their heads.

"Ah... brother!" he cried in response. For some reason he never called me by my name, but always said brother. I am ten years older than he. And he always listened carefully to what I said. "Wait, wait here," he continued, "by the little wood. We'll be back right away. I can't leave the troop."

At the edge of the wood, a little away from the dismounted troop, we smoked greedily. I was calm and insistent. Everything was madness. Mother was absolutely right.

I whispered to him, "As soon as you return from the village, come with me into town. Then get out of here and never come back."

"What are you saying, brother?"

"Be quiet," I said, "Be quiet. I know what I'm saying."

The troop had mounted. They were swaying, moving at a trot toward the billowing black smoke. In the distance a pounding began. Rapid, rapid pounding.

What could happen in just an hour? They would come back. I settled down to wait by the tent with the red cross on it.

———

An hour later I saw him. He also returned at a trot. But there was no troop. Only one horseman with a lance galloped on either side of him, and one of them, the one on the right, leaned towards my brother periodically, as if he were whispering something to him. Squinting into the sun, I watched the strange masquerade. He had left in a gray cap and was returning in a red one. The sun was setting. Only a black silhouette crowned with brightness remained. There was no hair and there was no forehead. Instead, there was a red crown with yellow spikes in clumps.

My brother, the horseman, wearing a ragged red crown, sat motionless on a lathered horse, and if the horseman on the right had not been carefully supporting him, he might have been on his way to a parade.

The horseman sat proud in the saddle, but he was blind and mute. There were two red blotches with streaks where an hour ago bright eyes had shone...

The horseman on the left dismounted, his left hand clutched the reins, but the one on the right very carefully led Kolya by the hand. Kolya swayed.

A voice said, "I'm afraid our volunteer... he's been hit by a shell fragment. Orderly, call a doctor..."

The other sighed and said, "Sure... but why call a doctor, buddy? Better a priest."

Then the black veil thickened and everything was obscured, even the head gear...

———

I have gotten used to everything. To this white building of ours, to the twilight, to the ginger cat who purrs at the door, but I cannot get used to his visits. The first time it happened, when I was still living downstairs in No. 63, he came out of the wall. He was wearing the red crown. There was nothing terrifying in that. I had seen him like that in dreams. But of course I knew that since he was wearing the crown he was dead. Then he spoke, moving his lips, which were caked with blood. He eased them apart, clicked his heels, put his hand to the crown in a salute, and said: "Brother, I can't leave the troop."

Since then it is always the same. He comes wearing his field shirt, with straps across his chest, with a curved saber and silent spurs, and says the same thing. Salute. Then: "Brother, I can't leave the troop."

You cannot imagine how it affected me the first time it happened! He gave the whole clinic a fright. Anyway, it is all over for me. It stands to reason that since he is wearing a halo, he has been killed, and if the dead come and talk to me, it means I have gone mad.

———

Yes. Now it's twilight. It is the hour of reckoning. But once I dozed off and saw the living room with the worn red velvet furniture. The comfortable armchair with a cracked leg. The portrait in a dusty black frame on the wall. Flowers on stands. The piano was open and on it was the score from *Faust*. He stood in the doorway, and a wild happiness warmed my heart. He was not a horseman. He was as he had been before those accursed days. In a black double-breasted jacket with a smudge of chalk on the elbow. His lively eyes smiled playfully and a lock of hair hung down over his forehead. He was nodding to me.

"Brother, let's go to my room. Do I have something to show you!..."

The rays from his eyes lit up the living room, and the burden of remorse melted inside me. That ill-fated day when I told him: "Go" had never existed, there was no pounding or acrid smoke. He had never gone away and had never been a horseman. He played the piano, the ivory keys tinkled, the golden rays of light touched everything, and his voice was expressive and he laughed.

———

Then I woke up. There was nothing. No light, no eyes. I never had that dream again. Then that very night, to compound my unbearable torture, he came anyway, stepping silently, the horseman in full military regalia, and he spoke to me the way he has decided to speak to me for eternity.

I decided to put an end to it. I said forcefully, "What are you, my eternal torturer? Why do you come? I admit everything. I take the blame for sending you on that doomed mission. I also take the blame for the hanging. Since I admit all this, forgive me and leave me alone."

I tell you, General, Sir, he said nothing and left.

So I became bitter from this torment and wished with all my might that he would come to you just once and put his hand to the crown in a salute. I assure you, you would be finished, just like me. At one stroke. However, perhaps you, too, are not alone at night? Who knows, perhaps you are visited by that soot-smeared man from the lamppost in Berdyansk? If this is so, we suffer it as we must. I sent Kolya to help you carry out the hanging, but you were the one who actually did it. By verbal order.

So, he did not leave. Then I scared him away with a scream. Everyone woke up. The attendant came running, they woke Ivan Vasilievich. I could not face the next day, but they wouldn't let me do myself in. They bound me with canvas straps, tore the glass from my hands, and bandaged me. Since then I have been in No. 27. After I was drugged I began to doze off, and heard the attendant talking in the corridor:

"A hopeless case."

———

It's true. I have no hope. Futilely, in burning anguish, I wait in the twilight for the dream to come—that old familiar room and the peaceful light from those radiant eyes. But all of that is gone forever.

The burden does not ease. And at night I wait submissively for the familiar horseman with the sightless eyes to come and say hoarsely: "I can't leave the troop."

Yes, I am hopeless. He will drive me to my grave.

1922

The Night of the Third

In the blinding light of a street lamp the Cossack officer sparkled with hoarfrost, like Father Christmas, and he yelled out in a strange language composed of a mixture of Russian, Ukrainian, and words he put together himself, the Cossack leader.

"For Christ's fucking sake!! Take off your boots, I'm tell you! Take'em off, swine! And if you ain't froze, then shoot you, for God's sake, you mother!!"

The Cossack officer waved his Mauser, aimed it at the star of Venus hanging over Slobodka, and pulled the trigger. Lightning streaked five times, five times a din rang out from the Cossack officer's hand, deafeningly cheerful, and five times, somersaulting happily—trakh—takh—akh—takh—dakh into the ice-covered spans the playful echo shot out.

Then they threw the future privat docent and qualified specialist, Doctor Bakaleinikov, off the bridge. The soldiers rushed ahead like a senseless herd, the hospital gowns they wore pressed forward like a black wall, the decayed parapet wheezed, cracked open, and Doctor Bakaleinikov, crying plaintively, fell like a sack of oats.

So—snow is cold. But from the height of the six meters from the bridge into the fathomless snowdrift—it's hot, like boiling water.

Doctor Bakaleinikov rose up, like a penknife, and tested the thin crust of ice over the snow. Raising up two meters of burning white cloud, he disappeared up to his neck. Gasping, he collapsed on his side even deeper, and with inhuman strength he flung up a second cloud, felt the boiling water on his cheeks and behind his collar, and by some miracle he climbed out. First he felt it on his chest, then on his knees, on his ankles (boiling water in his underpants) and, finally—the hard ice-covered slope.

On it the doctor, completely against his will, did a gigantic pirouette, scraped his left hand against the barbed wire until it bled, and sat right down on the ice.

Twice the Mauser rang out from the bridge, and rumbling and stamping began to rage. And above the ground the divine velvet night was shining in diamond splashes.

The doctor turned his face, with its snow-white furry eyelashes, to the twinkling stars, and he began to give his speech to the stars, spitting snow from his mouth, "I—am a fool. I—am a pitiful bastard."

Tears appeared in the doctor's eyes, and he continued, addressing the stars and the yellow blinking lights of Slobodka.

"Fools must be taught. So that's what I need."

With his numb hand he began to pull a handkerchief from the pocket of his pants. He pulled it out and wound it around his hand. A black stripe appeared on the cloth. The doctor continued, fixing his gaze on the magical sky:

"Lord. If you exist, make the Bolsheviks appear in Slobodka this minute. This minute."

Absorbed by the inviting yellow lights in the little flattened houses, the doctor breathed a very deep sigh...

"I—am a monarchist by conviction. But right now we need the Bolsheviks. Hell! It's oozing ... it's really skinned. Ah, the scoundrels! Lord... make the Bolsheviks come out of the dark blackness beyond Slobodka and land on the bridge."

The doctor hissed voluptuously, imagining sailors in black pea-coats. They'd fly in like a hurricane, and the Ukrainian forces' hospital gowns would fly in all directions. The Cossack officer and that vile monkey in a scarlet hat—Colonel Mashchenko—would be all that's left. They would both fall to their knees.

"Have pity, kind sir," they'd wail.

But Doctor Bakaleinikov steps forward and says:

"No, comrades! No. I—am a monar... No, that's not necessary... But it's like this: I am against the death penalty. Yes. Against. Karl Marx, I admit, I haven't read, and I don't even quite understand what connection he has with all this mess, but these two we've got to kill, like rabid dogs. They're scum. Vile pogrom organizers and thieves."

"Ah—ah—... so..." ominously answer the sailors.

And Doctor Bakaleinikov continues:

"Yes,—c-c-comrades. I'll shoot them myself!"

The doctor has a sailor's revolver in his hands. He aims. At the head. One. At the head. The other.

Then the snow behind his collar melted, a chill ran down his spine, and Doctor Bakaleinikov came to his senses. All covered in powdered snow, sparkling and glistening, he crawled along the slope back onto the bridge. His arm jerked unbearably, and bells rang in his head.

The black hospital gowns formed a semicircle. Gray crowds ran in front of them and vanished in mysterious Slobodka. Two steps away from the machine gun, on the trampled snow, sat a soldier without his hat who was stupidly looking at the ground and taking off his shoes. The Cossack officer, his left hand on his hip, waved the Mauser in his right hand in time to his words: "Take them off, take them off, you bore," he said.

On his round pimpled face was cold determination. Ukrainians with basins on their heads looked at the soldier with open mouths. Burning curiosity shone in their flickering eyes.

The soldier fumbled around for a long time. Finally he took off his boot with the hole. Under the boot was a hard blue-black foot cloth. The leaden year and a half passed over the doctor while the soldier was untying the disgusting rag.

"He'll kill him... kill him..." rang in his head—"this fool's still got his feet. Lord, why is he quiet?"

Something like a sigh or a hum broke out from the Ukrainians.

Finally, the soldier threw off the disgusting rag; slowly, with both hands, he raised his leg right up to the Cavalry leader's nose. His white, completely frozen gnarled foot stuck out.

A somber cloud of perplexity wiped the determination from the Cavalry officer's round face. And his white eyelashes blinked.

"To the infirmary. Let him go!"

The hospital gowns made way, and the soldier went onto the bridge, hobbling. Doctor Bakaleinikov watched as a man with a bare foot carried in his hands his boot and a pile of rags, and burning envy tore at his heart. To be behind him! There. Here he is—and the city's there! St. Vladimir's cross glitters on the hills beyond the river, and in the sky lies the pale phosphorescent reflection of the streetlights. Home. Home. My God! Oh, peace! Oh, heavenly rest!

A wild scream rang out suddenly from the white building. A scream, then a sigh. A scream.

"They're beating a Yid," a fruity, quiet voice tinkled.

Bakaleinikov froze in the icy powder, and before his eyes flickered a white wall and black eyesockets with broken glass or a wide-cheekboned something, vaguely resembling a human face, covered with a gray German basin.

It was as if they were beating a rug in the building. And a scream expanded, rising to the point that it seemed as if all of Slobodka was filled with the howl of a thousand people.

"What's that?" someone's voice yelled out clear and sharp. Only when the wide-cheekboned image was right next to Bakaleinikov's own eyes did he realize that the voice was his own, and he clearly understood as well that if there were another second of human wailing, he, with a light and happy heart, would thrust his fingernails into the wide-cheekbone's mouth and tear it to bloody pieces. The something, opening his eyes as wide as possible, faded backwards into the fog.

"What are you beating him for?!"

The future privat docent avoided irreparable disaster only because the din from the bridge drowned out the scream and the blows, and the whirlpool twirled around the mug in the helmet and Bakaleinikov himself.

A new crowd of deserters, Ukrainian soldiers, and haidamaks,[1] was pouring down from the mouth of Slobodka to the bridge. The Cavalry officer, moving back, sent four bullets over their heads into the black estuary.

"Blue Division! Show yourself!" Colonel Mashchenko's voice rang out like a rattle. A hat with a crimson top flew up, a stallion squeezed by the black

1. Haidamak historically refers to Ukrainian Cossacks, but here the Ukrainian nationalist cavalry detachment is meant, as distinct from the Infantry, simply referred to here as soldiers—all, however, belonging to the Ukrainian Nationalist forces.

hospital gowns, snorting from the bristle of bayonets, stood up on his hind legs.

"Forward march!"

The black battalion of the Blue Division crashed out with the crackle of a hundred feet and moved out between the pincers of its mounted officers, crushing the remains of a temporary wooden parapet, it sank into the black estuary and drove the senseless soldiers in front of it. In the din was a muffled voice:

"Long live Batko Petliura!!"[2]

———

Oh, the star-filled, dear Ukrainian nights. Oh, peace and divine rest!..

———

At nine o'clock, when the black unit swept the respected doctor and everything else in front of it to the devil, in the town beyond the river, in Doctor Bakaleinikov's own apartment, there was the usual peace of objects and confusion of souls. Varvara Afanasievna—the doctor's wife—rushed about from one black window to the next, and kept looking out as if she wanted to make out her husband and Slobodka in the black thicket which had so few lights.

2. Simon Petliura was the Ukrainian nationalist leader whose forces took Kiev in early 1919.

Kolka Bakaleinikov and Yury Leonidovich followed on her heels.

"Stop it Varya! What are you all excited for? Nothing's happened to him. He's a fool for going, it's true, but I think he's got enough sense to get away."

"For God's sake, nothing's going to happen," asserted Yury Leonidovich, and the greased feathers of his hair stood on end.

"You're just trying to calm me!... They'll take him off to Galicia."

"What do you mean, for God's sake. He'll come."

"Varvara Afanasievna!!"

"All right, I'll accompany you... My God! What's that scummy thing? What's with the feathers? What, have you gone crazy? Where's your part?"

"Hee-hee. He's got a haircut *à la* the Bolsheviks."

"Nothing of the sort," lied Yury Leonidovich, blushing a deep color.

This, however, was the absolute truth. Towards evening, upon leaving Jean the barber's who, for two months under Petliura worked under the mysterious sign "Goliarnia," Yury Leonidovich had begun to yawn, watching Petliura's men with their red tails run off to the station by car, and he collided with some kind of black shirt. Yury Leonidovich—to the right, and the other to the right, left and left... Finally, they passed.

"Just think, a Ukrainian lord! Takes up half the side-walk. They'll take his sticks with the golden knobs for the common pot."

Pensively and attentively Yury Leonidovich turned around, measured the black greasy spine with a glance, smiled as if he'd read some letters on it, and muttered: "It isn't worth getting mixed up in it. Congratulations. By night the Bolsheviks will be in the city."

Therefore, when he got home he decided to change his appearance, and he did an amazing job. Instead of his very proper jacket there appeared a sweater with a hole in the stomach; the cane with the golden knob was left in his mother's keeping. A flap-eared rag replaced his beaver cap. And the devil knows what was on his head under the rag. Yury Leonidovich watered the construction from Jean of "Goliarnia" and combed his hair back. It would have been okay, but when it dried and puffed up... Lord!

"Take it away! I'm not going to accompany you. The devil knows what you look like... a Papuan!"

"A Comanche. A chief—Hawk Eye."

Yury Leonidovich humbly lowered his head.

"All right. I'll do my hair over."

"I think—you'd better do it over! Kolka, take him to your room."

When they returned Yury Leonidovich no longer looked like a Comanche, but was, as before, a smoothly coiffed former guards' officer, at present a pupil of Makrushin's opera studio, and the possessor of a phenomenal baritone.

> *Beauteous city... happy ci-i-ty!*
> *The tsarina of the seas, the glorious Vedenets*
> *Qui-i-etly flutters about...*

Velvet lava filled the living room and softened the hearts filled with anxiety.

> *Oh Ci-i-i-i-ty di-i-vine!!*

The ringing lava filled the room completely, thundering in countless reverberations from the walls and the quivering panes of glass. And only when the smooth-haired Comanche, having muffled the sound towering over the subjugated chords, brought out an amazing *mezzo-voce*:

> *The moon is shi-i-i-ning from the night sky!...*

did Kolka and Varvara Afanasievna hear the diabolically terrifying peal of the basins.

The chord broke off, but *do* still sounded with the pedal, the voice broke off too, and Kolka jumped up as if he'd been stung.

"I'll bet my life it's Vasilisa! Him, him, curse him!"

"My God..."

"Oh, calm down..."

"I'll bet my life. How can the earth endure such a coward?"

Behind the window floated an unearthly din, unrolling in confusion. Kolka began to rush about, pushing a revolver into his pocket.

"Kolya, get rid of that Browning! Kolya, I'm begging you..."

"Lord, don't get so scared!"

The door in the dining room banged, then the one on the veranda going out into the yard. The din burst into the room for a minute. In the yard, alongside the yard, and further down the entire street the jam basins rang out. A booming, rocking, alarming crash poured out, shaking the frosty air.

"Kolya, don't leave the yard. Yury Leonidovich don't let him!"

But the door slammed, they both disappeared, and from behind the door floated a deafening... Dong, dong... dong....

Kolka had guessed it. Vasilisa—landlord and bourgeois, gentleman and coward, was the reason for the alarm. It wasn't just on this frightening, troubled night, as they were waiting for Soviet rule to replace Petliura that poor Vasilisa lived in a state of continuous, chronic nightmare, but during the course of the entire year that the town had seen the most diverse rulers come and go. In this nightmare, alternating and in succession, he saw either the fierce faces of sailors with golden letters in their hero's ribbons, or white papers with blue inscriptions, or evil tails, or the mugs of German lieutenants wearing monocles. In his ears rang the shooting of rifles day and night, basins sounded, and the landlord Vasilisa turned into the chairman of the house committee and every morning while getting up, the poor devil waited for some new, extraordinary surprise, a surprise to everybody. But most of all, he waited to the point that he lost his own first, middle, and last names—Vasily Ivanovich Lisovich—and became Vasilisa.

On the countless scraps of paper and questionnaires, which every new government required by the pile, the house committee chairman began to write—Vas. Lis. and a long, trembling flourish. This was all in expectation of some kind of terrifying, exceptional responsibility for the coming—as yet unknown—but, according to the housing committee chairman, punishing power.

There wasn't anything more to say, just that when Kolka Bakaleinikov received the first sugar ration card signed Vas. and Lis., the whole yard began to call the landlord Vasilisa, and then all his acquaintances in the town as well. So the name Vasily Ivanovich was only used in the rare case of talking to Vasilisa directly.

Kolka, assuming the role of the house committee secretary for the records of the house guard, could not deny himself the pleasure on the great night of the third of assigning Vasilisa duty with the shortest, pudgiest woman on the block, Avdotia Semyonovna—the shoemaker's wife. So in the timetable it read—the 2nd: from 8 to 10—Avdotia and Vasilisa.

Basically, it was a lot of fun. For a whole evening Kolka taught Vasilisa how to use an Austrian carbine. Vasilisa sat on a little bench under the wall, flabby, with downcast eyes, as Kolka used an extractor to toss out cartridges and tried to hit Vasilisa with them.

Finally, having enjoyed himself to his fill, he fastened a copper bucket for cooking to a branch of the acacia with his own hand (to sound the alarm) and left, leaving the completely motionless Vasilisa with the sullen Avdotia.

"You keep a look out, Vasil...is...Ivanovich—" Kolka threw out despondently in parting, "in case of anything... that... take aim—" and he winked ominously at the carbine.

Avdotia spit.

"This Petliura should just drop dead for the way he's upset people..."

Vasilisa stirred only one time after Kolka's departure. With his hands he carefully lifted the carbine by the muzzle and the gunstock, placed it under the bench with the muzzle on the side, and again sat still.

Despair seized Vasilisa at ten when the sounds of life began to die down in the city, and Avdotia categorically announced that she needed to absent herself for five minutes. The song of the Vedenets guest faintly emerged from behind the cream-colored blinds, and eased poor Vasilisa's heart just a bit. But only for a short minute. Just then, on the hill behind the fence, above the roof of the shed, which the garden, lightly covered with snow, approached in terraces, there was a very distinct shadow, and with a rustling a layer of snow caved in. Vasilisa closed his eyes and in the space of an instant he saw a whole series of scenes: bandits bursting forth, they were slitting Vasilisa's throat and he, Vasilisa, lay in a coffin dead. Weakly moaning, Vasilisa knocked twice on the bucket with a stick. Immediately they banged through the neighboring yard, then through another yard, and in a minute all of Andreevskaya Street was howling with copper, threatening voices, and immediately in Number 17 shooting began. Vasilisa, his legs spread, stiffened, holding the stick in his hands.

The moon was shining.

A door crashed and out jumped Kolka, holding his coat by the sleeves, and behind him Yury Leonidovich.

"What happened?"

Instead of an answer Vasilisa pointed, indicating the shed. Kolka and Yury Leonidovich carefully glanced at the gate to the yard. It was empty and silent, and Avdotia's tomcat had made off long ago, driven crazy by the diabolical noise.

"You were the first to strike?"

Vasilisa gasped convulsively, licked his lips, and answered:

"No, it seems it wasn't me..."

Kolka, turning aside, raised his eyes to the sky and whispered:

"Oh, what a man!"

Then he ran out through the gate and disappeared for a quarter of an hour. First they stopped clattering nearby, then in number 17, then in number 19, and then for a long, long time someone was still shooting at the end of the street, but even he finally stopped. And again there was an anxious silence.

Kolka, when he returned, stopped the torture of Vasilisa; with the powerful hand of the house committee secretary he called Drabinsky and his wife (10-12:00) and darted back to the house. Running into the hall on his tiptoes, Kolka took a breath and shouted in a prompter's whisper:

"Hooray! Rejoice, Varvara... Hooray! They're chasing Petliura out! The Reds are coming."

"What's this?"

"Listen... I just ran out to the street, I saw a transport. The tails are leaving, I'm telling you, leaving."

"You're not lying?"

"You crazy girl. Why would I?"

Varvara Afanasievna jumped from her armchair and said hastily:

"Will Mikhail really come back?"

"Yes, of course. I'm sure they've already broken out of Slobodka. Listen: as soon as they chase them out, where will they go? To the city, of course, across the bridge. When they cross through the city, then Mikhail will get away!"

"And if they don't let him go?"

"So-o... they don't let him go. You don't have to be a fool. He can just run away."

"That's clear," agreed Yury Leonidovich and ran to the piano. He sat down, poked at the keyboard with his finger, and began quietly:

> *Sol... do!..*
> *Branded, cursed...*

but Kolka, squeezing his mouth with his hands, imitated how soldiers yell "hooray."

"Ho-o-o-oray!..."

"You've both gone crazy! Petliura's men are on the street!..."

"Ho-o-o-oray!... Down with Petliu...ap!.."

Varvara Afanasievna rushed to Kolka and put her hand over his mouth.

———

Doctor Bakaleinikov saw the first murder of his life second by second on the turning point as the night of the second turned into the third. At midnight, near the entrance to the cursed bridge. Two Ukrainians were carrying a man with a black and blue face, stained with blood, in a torn overcoat, over the snow.

The Cavalry officer ran alongside and beat him on the spine with a ramrod. The head shook with each blow, but the bloodied man no longer screamed, but just cried out strangely. The rod came down heavy and sharp on the coat which was torn to shreds, and each strike was answered by a hoarse: "Ukh...a."

Bakaleinikov's legs became cotton wool, they bent, and snowy Slobodka rocked.

"Ah-h, your Jewish mug!" yelled the Cavalry officer in a frenzy, speaking half in Ukrainian, half in Russian. "Take him to the woodpile to be shot! I'll show you, skulking in dark corners! I'll show you! What'd you do behind the woodpile? What!?"

But the bloodied one didn't answer. Then the Cavalry officer ran up in front and the Ukrainian soldiers jumped aside, to avoid the flying, flashing cane. The Cavalry officer didn't calculate his blow but with lightning speed he lowered the rod on the head. Something crunched, and the black bloodied one now didn't even answer..ukh... Somehow strangely, twisting his arm and shaking his head, he collapsed over on his side from his knees and, waving wildly with his other hand, he cast it back as if he wanted to grab more of the trampled, manured, white earth.

Bakaleinikov could still distinctly see how his writhing fingers bent and raked the snow. Then, lying in a dark pool he jerked his lower jaw as if choking, and all at once went still.

Strangely, as if croaking, Bakaleinikov sobbed, and drunkenly reeling, walked on ahead, to the side of the bridge, to a white building. Raising his head to the sky he saw the hissing white streetlight, and higher still shone the black sky, girded by the pale shoulder belt of the Milky Way, and the sparkling stars. And at just that minute, when the prostrate black man gave up the ghost, the doctor saw a miracle in the sky. The star of Venus over Slobodka suddenly exploded in the frozen heights into a fiery dragon, it spurted fire and detonated deafeningly. The black distance, which for so long had tolerated villainy, came, finally, to the aid of weakened, pitifully helpless man. Behind the star the expanse emitted a frightful sound, a long and heavy thunder. And just then the second star clapped, but lower, right over the roofs buried under the snow.

...The soldiers ran in a gray herd. And there was no one to hold them back. The blue division ran in disorderly crowds, and the haidamaks' fur caps with tails danced over the black ribbon. The Cavalry officer disappeared, Colonel Mashchenko disappeared. Slobodka was left behind forever along with its yellow fires and with the bridge with its blinding chain of white lights. And the beautiful city, the happy city, poured out to meet the mountains.

———

Doctor Bakaleinikov suddenly escaped from the black ribbon by the white church with columns and, not feeling his heart, on strangely unbending legs, he went over to the side, right to the church. Nearer to the columns. Even nearer. His spine began to burn as if from a thousand looks. God, it's all boarded up! There isn't a soul. Where can I run? Where? And finally, something terrible from behind:

"Freeze!"

The column is nearer. His heart is gone.

"Freeze! Fre-eze!"

Then Doctor Bakaleinikov—a solid fellow—broke away and began running so fast that the wind whistled in his face.

"Hold him! Hold him!!"

One. Bang. One. Bang. Hit. Hit. Hit. The third column. The fourth. The fifth. Then the doctor accidentally saved his life by running into a side street. Otherwise, mounted haidamaks would have caught him in an instant on the illuminated, straight, boarded up Alexandrovskaya Street. But further on was a network of crooked black side streets. Farewell!

———

Doctor Bakaleinikov pressed into a crack in the wall. For a minute he expected to die from a heart seizure and he swallowed the burning air. He scattered to the winds the certificate saying he'd been mobilized in the capacity of a doctor "in the first rank of the blue division" of Petliura's army. In case he met the first Red patrol in the empty town.

———

Around 3 a.m. in Doctor Bakaleinikov's apartment a deafening ring broke out.

"Hey, I told you!" Kolka yelled, "stop bellowing! Stop..."

"Varvara Afanasievna! It's him. Come, come."

Kolka broke away and flew to open the door.

"Oh, dear God!"

Varvara Afanasievna threw herself at Bakaleinikov and then recoiled.

"You, you... you're gray..."

Bakaleinikov dully looked into the mirror and smiled crookedly, twitching his cheek. Then, frowning, he pulled off his coat with Kolka's help and, without a word he went into the dining room, sat down on a chair, and then slumped over like a sack. Varvara Afanasievna glanced at him and the tears again began to fall from her eyes. Yury Leonidovich and Kolka, their mouths open, looked at the back of Bakaleinikov's head and at the white forelock, and both their cigarettes went out.

Bakaleinikov ran his eyes over the quiet dining room, his lackluster gaze stopping on the samovar for a few seconds as he looked at his distorted reflection in its shiny side.

"Yes," he finally managed to get out, senselessly. Kolka hearing this, his first word, decided to ask:

"Listen, you... ran, right? So tell us what you did with them."

"You know," Bakaleinikov answered slowly, "they, just imagine, wore hospital gowns, these same blue Petliurists. In black..."

Bakaleinikov wanted to say something else, but instead of words something unexpected happened. He sobbed loudly, sobbed again some more, and then broke down like a woman, burying his head with its gray forelock in his arms. Varvara Afanasievna, not knowing what was going on, cried out at the same second. Yury Leonidovich and Kolka got so upset they even became pale. Kolka collected himself first and dashed to the cabinet for tincture of valerian, and clearing his throat, Yury Leonidovich said something apparently illogical:

"Yes, he's scum, that Petliura."

Bakaleinikov raised his face which was distorted from crying, and still sobbing, he cried out:

"Gangsters!.. But I... I... intelligentsia garbage!—" also apparently illogical.

And the scent of ether spread. With trembling hands Kolka began to count drops into a glass.

———

In an hour the town was sleeping. Doctor Bakalei-nikov was sleeping. The streets, boarded doorways, and closed gates were silent. There wasn't a single person on the streets. And the distance was silent as well. Not a sound came from the river, from Slobodka with its anxious yellow fires, or from the bridge with its pale chain of streetlights. And the black ribbon which had crossed the city disappeared in the darkness on the other side. The sky hung like a velvet bedcurtain with diamond fragments, Venus, miraculously stuck back together, again glittered over Slobodka, almost reddish, and there lay the white shoulder belt—the silvery Milky Way.

1922

Feuilletons

Red Stone Moscow

Annushka[1] hums, clangs, clatters, and sways. She speeds along the Kremlin Embankment to the Cathedral of the Savior.

It is pleasant at the cathedral. Such a bulky bit of air hung over the Moscow River, stretching from the white walls to the four ugly, smokeless stacks sticking up from Zamoskvorechie.[2]

Behind the church where bulky Alexander III once sat majestically in state wearing soft accordion boots there is now only an empty pedestal. A cumbersome commode which has nothing on it and for which there is apparently nothing intended. And above the pedestal a column of air rising into the blue sky.

As much space as you want.

It is overwhelming, I don't know where to begin.

In winter the massive steps leading from the monument became icy and disappeared under the snow. Boys, selling loose "Java" tobacco, slid down the snowy slope on sleds and hurled snowballs at Annushka as she hurried past. But in summer the flagstones around the church and the steps at the pedestal are bare. Two figures come into view and descend to the streetcar line. One of them has a green hump strapped to his

1. Meaning, the streetcar.
2. Historical region of Moscow situated on the right bank of the Moscow River south of the Kremlin.

back. The hump contains rations. In the winter half of Moscow went around with humps. The humps were dragged along behind them on sleds. But now it's over. No more civilian rationing. You get millions of rubles and flock to the stores.

The other figure does not have a hump. He's well-dressed. Starched white shirt and striped trousers. On his head is a velvet hatband faded by storms and tempests. On the hatband is a golden emblem. Not exactly a hammer and spade, nor a sickle and rake, but definitely not a hammer and sickle. A Red specialist.[3] He's employed by something like KhMU[4] or the Central Supply Administration. He is fortunate, he does not want for anything. Every day he walks along Tverskaya and enters the huge store, Empeo, which in legendary times was Elyseev's, and pokes his finger at the glass, behind which lies the treasure.

"Hey... two pounds..."

The shop assistant in a white apron, "Right away... sir..."

He makes a quick sharp cut with his knife, but not on the piece at which the specialist pointed, which is a little fresher, but from the one next to it, which looks more suspect.

"Please pay the cashier..."

3. A pre-revolutionary specialist (technocrat) who is now on the Communist payroll since there are few Communists with the required expertise as engineers, scientists, managers, etc.

4. Supply and Equipment Bureau of the People's Commissariat for Rail Transport.

Chit. The young lady holds his bill up to the light. All bills are examined in this way. Everyone has to be cautious. Although no one in Moscow knows what they are looking for. The cash register clatters, thunders, and swallows the specialist's ten million. In change, two one-hundred notes.

One is watermarked and genuine, and the other, also watermarked, is counterfeit.

In the Empeo, in the Elyseev's plate-glass windows, there is a constant flow of shoppers. Three pounds. Five pounds. Black caviar glistens in jars. Smoked salmon. Pyramids of apples and oranges. Some masochist presses his nose to the window and gazes wide-eyed at the chandeliers, oranges, and bunches of grapes. His head reels. Had he slept through the years 1918-22?!

Cyclist after cyclist rides along the worn-out wooden pavement. Motorcycles. Automobiles. They whistle and caw as if a machine gun is firing. They run on auto-cognac gasoline. You pour it into the car and start up—then the car lays a plume of stifling, blue-gray smoke.

Plucked, stripped, and dilapidated cars speed by. Some drivers have briefcases, some wear helmets with red stars, and suddenly you see a lady in a fur stole and hundred-million-ruble hat from Kuznetsky Street bobbing up and down on leather cushions. And next to her, of course, a faded hatband. A nouveau riche. A Nepman.

Sometimes a noiseless car flashes by, waxed and gleaming. In it is a foreign gentleman. American Relief Administration.

There are cabs, sometimes a string of them, sometimes just one. The raging storm did not touch them. They are the same as they were in 1822 and will be the same in 2022, if horses are not extinct by then. They are rude to those who bargain and obsequious with the nouveau riche.

"I seem to remember you, sir!"

The ordinary Soviet public, the kaleidoscopic mass of diversified faces that the Moscow conductresses call citizens (stress on the second syllable), travels by streetcar.

God knows where they come from and who repairs them, but there are more and more of them all the time. They are already clanking along fourteen routes in Moscow. Most of the time there is no room to stand, sit, or lie down. However, there are times when they are less crowded. There is Annushka turning in under the clock at Prechistensky Gates. Inside are a conductor, conductress, and three passengers. At first, three people waiting at the next stop automatically form a line. But suddenly the line disintegrates. Their faces become anxious. They begin shoving each other with their elbows. One grabs for the left rail, the other simultaneously for the right. Instead of simply getting on they "push in." They storm the empty car. Why? What does it mean? This phenomenon has already been studied. Atavism. They remember the times when no one stood, but hung on instead. When heavy bags rode along with the people. Now try it! Try pushing your way onto a streetcar at Yaroslav Station with a bag weighing 180 pounds.

"Citizens, no baggage allowed."

"What are you talking about... it's only a little tiny bundle."

"Citizen! It's not allowed!! Can't you get it through your head?!"

A bell. Stop. You are thrown off.

And: "Citizens, get your tickets. Citizens, move down."

The citizens move down, the citizens get their tickets. The citizens are wearing whatever they've got. Blouses, shirts, field jackets, and suit coats. Mostly there are field jackets, loathsome clothing, a reminder of the war. Caps, visored field caps. Short leather jackets. The majority wear disreputable, worn-out, down-at-the-heel shoes. But there are already some patent leather shoes. Laid-off Soviet young ladies⁵ wearing white shoes.

The kaleidoscopic masquerade rides the streetcar.

There is hubbub and uproar at the streetcar stops. Hoarse alto ventriloquists sing, "Tooday's *Izvestiya-a*... Patriarch Tikhkhkhkha-a-an!... Socialist revolutionaries... *Nakannu-une*⁶... just in from Burlin."

5. A pejorative euphemism for girl employees in the Soviet offices who were willing to enter into liasons with speculators and high Soviet officials and thereby obtain flour and sugar, or even cosmetics and silk stockings.

6. An emigre periodical published in Berlin, in which many of Bulgakov's feuilletons appeared, including this one.

The streetcar rushes into the midst of the noise, hubbub, and honking. Into the center of the city.

It flies past Moskovskaya Street. Billboard after billboard. A yard of them. A mile of them. The fresh paint strikes the eye. You can find everything in them. Everything is there except the hard signs and yats.[7] Tsupvoz. Tsustran. Mosselprom. Decoding their meaning. Mosdrevotdel. Vinotorg. Staro-Rykovsky tavern. The tavern has been resurrected but has lost its hard sign. "Sport Tavern." "Workers' theater." That's right. Those who work need to relax at the theater. "Sandel" manufacturer. Sandals, no doubt. Women's, children's, and "boy" shoes. Vryvsel promgvnu Unitorg, Mostorg and glavlestorg. Tsentrobumtrest.[8]

Against the kaleidoscopic jumble of words and letters on a black background is a white figure, a skeleton stretching its arms skyward. Help! F-a-m-i-n-e. In a wreath of thorns, framed by a mane of hair, there is a girl's face veiled by the shadows of death, with eyes which express the anguish of starvation. Children with swollen bellies and adult skeletons with skin stretched over their bones are scattered on the ground. You take a good look. You contemplate it and the joy goes out of

7. Names of letters declared obsolete and eliminated by the language reform of 1917-18.

8. In this paragraph Bulgakov is making untranslatable fun of the Soviet acronyms which sprang up in these years. Decoded, they are such things as: Central Directorate for Military Procurement; Association of Establishments for the Processing of Products from the Agricultural Industry; Association of Woodworking Industry Facilities in the Moscow Region; and Main Trade Administration, Executive Committee, Moscow City Council of Labor Deputies, etc.

your day. However, those who had enough to eat the whole time do not understand this. The nouveau riche rush past and don't bother to look...

The street is noisy until late at night. And the urchins, red merchants, are doing business. The hands on the round lighted clock crawl towards two, but Tverskoi Boulevard still shows signs of life, tosses and turns and yelps. Violins quiver in the Cuckoo Cafe. But their playing becomes softer and intermittent. The windows down the side streets darken. Moscow sleeps at the close of a kaleidoscopic weekday before a Red holiday.

...When he goes to bed at night, the specialist prays to an Unknown God: "You can do it so easily. Send a cloudburst tomorrow. With hail. It's hailing heavily somewhere, why not here. Surely you can spare us some."

And he fantasizes: "I can just see it, there they are marching out with their placards, when all of a sudden from above 'kaboom'..."

The rain comes, and plenty of it. It gushes out of rusty drainpipes. But it rains at an absurd time that is of no use to anyone, at night. And in the morning the sky is crystal clear!

At the gate one woman says to another, "It looks like someone up there likes the Bolsheviks."

"It looks that way, dearie..."

At ten o'clock a deafening march rolls along Tverskaya. Company after company of Red infantry, wearing new field shirts with red chevrons and red, blue, and orange flaps on the front, in identical helmets, marches to the sound of clashing cymbals and blaring trumpets past dazzling shop windows and walls covered with faded red flags.

Sporting bicolored troop emblems the colorful cavalry trots by. Armored cars pass.

In the evening the boulevards are crowded. Alexander Sergeevich Pushkin, inclining his head,[9] attentively regards Tverskoi Boulevard buzzing at his feet. What he is thinking is anybody's guess... At night the lighted signs glow. The stars...

...And again Moscow sleeps. It is three by the lighted clock. In the silence, every quarter of an hour all of Moscow can hear a mysterious, gentle chime from the old tower at whose base stands a vigilant guard and a lamp which burns all night. A chime rings out from the Kremlin walls every quarter hour. And the street sleeps before a new work day for the extraordinary, unprecedented commercial Red Kitai Gorod.[10]

1922

9. There is a statue of Pushkin located on the Tverskoi Boulevard.

10. The walled inner city on one side of the Kremlim marking ancient Moscow's first line of defenses. Literally, it means Chinatown.

The Capital in a Notebook

I

The Repair God

Every god has his own style. Mercury, for example has little wings on his feet. He is a Nepman and a rogue. But my favorite god is the Repair God who took up residence in Moscow in 1922. He wore an apron, was smeared with lime, and smelled of cheap makhorka tobacco. I too was touched by his brush, and to this day I have kept the mark of his divine touch on my fall coat, which I also wear in winter. Why? Oh yes, abroad they probably do not know that an entire class of Muscovites considers it fashionable to go about in their fall coats in winter. To this class belong the so-called creative intelligentsia and the intelligentsia of the future, those attending workers' schools and the like. The latter, however, do not even wear coats but a kind of short jacket. Cold?...

Nonsense. One easily gets used to it.

And so, it was the golden autumn when I and my pal, a specialist, came out of the hotel. The splendid god was ferociously working away. Scaffolding was up, white streams were running down the walls and it smelled deliciously of oil paint.

And that was where he smeared me, too.

The specialist greedily breathed in the smell of paint and said proudly, "Don't you love it. Just wait, in another year you won't recognize Moscow. Now 'we' (stress on this word) will show you what we can do!"

Unfortunately, the specialist did not have time to show anyone anything, because a week later he became a victim of the "Bolshevik terror." To be precise, they put him in Butyrki Prison.

The reason why is a complete mystery.

His wife said something incoherent regarding this: "It's an outrage! Do they have a signature? No? Let them show me the signature. That Sidorov (or Ivanov, I don't remember) is a scoundrel! He says twenty billion. First of all, it was fifteen."

Indeed, there is no signature (after all the specialist was not an idiot), so he will soon be released. And then he will really be able to show what he can do. Having gathered his strength in Butyrki Prison.

With or without the specialist, the Repair God remained. Perhaps because no matter how many specialists were imprisoned, an incredible number are still left (My statistics are accurate, there are 1,000,000 in Moscow, not one less!), or because it is possible to manage without specialists, but the splendid, indefatigable god—plasterer, painter, and bricklayer—is working away. Even now he is not at rest, although winter is already here and a soft snow is falling.

At the corner of Lubyanka and Myasnitskaya Streets, there was God knows what—some gnawed out bald spot covered with smashed brick and broken bottles. Now there is a building there. Admittedly it is only one story, but it is a building all the same! A *building!* Unbroken windows. Everything is as it should be. True, there is nothing inside yet, but on the outside a sign in gold letters already hangs out in splendor, spelling "knitwear."

Miracles are routinely happening right before our eyes. Yawning doorways on lower floors suddenly boast glass doors. In two days the windows will display glowing lamps, and cascades of fabric—or someone's head bent over papers—will appear under a green lampshade. I don't know why or whose head, but I can tell you what he is doing without looking inside. He is compiling the payroll list for overtime.

I will say quite frankly that the fabric is a good thing, but the head is not necessary. They just write and write... But obviously nothing can be done about it.

I believe that, in the end, fabric and kitchenware, umbrellas and galoshes will completely crowd out the balding heads of petty clerks. The Moscow landscape will become exquisite. To my taste.

I now walk with a feeling of delight through the arcades. At twilight Petrovka and Kuznetsky glow with lights. And there is a spectrum of luxuriant color in the windows, the faces of handcrafted toys smile.

The elevators are working! I saw them myself today. Can I believe my own eyes?

This season they are renovating, plastering, and painting. Next season, I believe, they will be building. In the autumn, looking at the asphalt boilers in the streets as they glowed with a hellish flame, I trembled with a joyful premonition. They will build, no matter what. It could be that this is the fantasy of an ardent Muscovite... But, say what you will, I see a Renaissance.

Moscow epithalamium:

"I sing to you, Oh Repair God!"

II

The Rotten Intelligentsia

I last saw him in June. At that time he came to see me, rolled a makhorka cigarette and said gloomily, "Well, I graduated from the university."

"Congratulations, doctor," I answered sincerely.

The prospects for a new doctor unfolded in the following manner. At the Department of Medicine he was told, "You are free to leave." In the med-student dormitory he was told, "Well, you've graduated now, so move out." In the clinics, hospitals, and similar institutions he was told, "We've cut back our staff."

The end result was utter gloom.

After that he disappeared and sank into the Moscow abyss.

"So, he's perished," I calmly noted, preoccupied with my own personal affairs, the so-called "struggle for survival."

I struggled as far as November and was preparing to struggle on when he unexpectedly appeared. From his shoulders still hung the threadbare rag (his former student coat), but brand new trousers could be seen beneath it.

From the single crease, aristocratically pressed, I could determine without a doubt that they had been bought in Sukharyovka[1] for seventy-five million!

He pulled out a syringe case and treated me to an "Ira"[2] cigarette.

Overcome by amazement, I waited for an explanation. It followed shortly.

"I work as a loader in an artel.[3] It's a nice artel, you know, six fifth-year students and me..."

"What on earth do you load?"

"Furniture for stores. We even have permanent clients."

"So, how much do you earn?"

"Well, last week I made 275 mil."

1. A huge slum area in Moscow notorious for its gambling, prostitution, and flea market.

2. A fancy grade of tobacco.

3. A cooperative association of workers and craftsmen working together under the guidance of an elected head.

I instantly multiplied: 275 x 4 = one billion one hundred thousand. A month!

"What about medicine?"

"That goes without saying. We load once or twice a week. The rest of the time I'm at the clinic. I take x-rays ."

"Do you have a room?"

He chuckled.

"Yes, I even have a room... it was strange, you know, the way it happened... we were delivering some furniture to a performer's apartment. She asks me with surprise, 'Who in fact are you, may I ask? You have such an intelligent face.' 'I'm a doctor,' I say. You should have seen what she did then!... She poured tea and asked me questions. 'Tell me, where do you live?' 'I don't have a place to live,' I say. She took such an interest, God bless her. And it was through her that I got the room, at some acquaintances' of hers. On one condition, that I don't get married."

"What, the artist set such a condition?"

"Why the artist... the landlords. They said they would rent to one person, but under no circumstances to two."

Enthralled by the fairy-tale successes of my friend, I said, after a moment's thought, "This is what they have all been writing about, the rotten intelligentsia, rotten... But really it's already died. After the Revolution a new, iron intelligentsia arose. It can even load furniture, and chop firewood, and take x-rays.

"I predict," I continued, lapsing into a lyrical tone, "it will not perish! It will survive."

He confirmed this, sending out suffocating puffs from his "Ira" cigarette: "Why perish? We refuse to perish."

III

A Boy In A Million

Yesterday morning I saw a boy on Tverskaya. An open-mouthed group of amazed men and women followed him, and a string of empty cabs stretched out behind as if following a casket.

Passengers leaned out of streetcar No. 6, coming in the opposite direction, and pointed at the boy. I will not swear to it, but it seemed that the woman selling apples outside building No. 73 started to sob with joy, and a rubbernecking driver cut a corner and miraculously escaped arrest.

I rubbed my eyes, not believing what I was seeing.

The boy did not have a tray with toffee slung from his shoulders, and the boy was not yelling at the top of his lungs, "Ambassadors! Java! Mursal!* Outofmyway-newspapercartisgoingtoflatteneveryone!..."

The boy did not grab crumpled million-ruble notes from some other boy and kick him. The boy did not

4. Three brands of cigarettes.

have a cigarette in his mouth... The boy did not use foul language. The boy did not get onto the steetcar in gaudy rags and make a show of running up to the well-groomed faces of profiteers and saying in a nasal twang, "Give me something... for Christ's sake..."

No, citizens. This one boy, the first I have met, was walking along, swaying with an unhurried, measured stride, wearing a splendid, cosy hat with earflaps, and his face displayed the virtues that only a boy of eleven or twelve possesses.

No, it was not a boy. It was a genuine cherub in warm gloves and felt boots. And on the cherub's back was a satchel from which protruded the corner of a math workbook.

The boy was going to elementary school to *study.*

Enough. Period.

IV

The Trillionaire

I went to visit some Nepmen I know. I was tired of visiting writers. Bohemia is good only in Murger,[5] the red wine, the women... Moscow's literary Bohemia, however, is depressing.

You arrive, and they either ask you to sit on a crate bristling with rusty nails, or there is no tea, or there is tea but no sugar, or the landlady is making moonshine

5. Henri Murger (1822-61). French writer, known for sketches of bohemian life in Paris.

vodka in the next room into which puffy-faced people sneak, and you sit there anxiously because you are afraid they will come and arrest the puffy-faced people and grab you as well, or, worst of all, young poets begin reading their poems. One, then a second, then a third... In short, an insufferable situation.

It turned out to be extremely pleasant at the homes of the Nepmen. There is tea, lemons, cookies, a house maid, silver spoons (note for the incredulous foreigner—my admiration is purely platonic), the smell of perfume is everywhere, the daughter plays "The Maiden's Prayer" on the piano, there is a divan, "Would you care for cream?" no one reads poems, etc.

The only problem is that looking at your reflection you notice that the small tear in your trousers is turning into a gaping hole the size of a saucer, and you have to cover it with your palm and stir your tea with your left hand. And the hostess says with a charming smile, "You are very nice and interesting, but why don't you buy yourself some new trousers? And while you're about it, a hat as well..."

After this "while you're about it" I choked on the tea and the scrofulous "Maiden's Prayer" seemed like a *danse macabre*.

But the doorbell rang and saved me.

Someone entered before whom everything paled and even the silver spoons curled up and looked like old tin.

There was something on the finger of the new guest that resembled the cross on the Cathedral of the Savior at sunset.

"Ninety carats... he must have taken it from a crown," whispered my neighbor, a poet, a man who in his poems sings the praises of precious stones, but who in his utter poverty has no idea what a carat is.

By the stone, which scattered multicolored rays in every direction, by the fact that the guest's fat wife wore a russet fur stole around her shoulders, and by the fact that the guest's eyes darted about shiftily, I guessed that before me was the Nepman of all Nepmen, who was also probably from a trust.[6]

The hostess blushed, flashed her gold crowns in a smile, and rushed to meet them with a cry, interrupting "The Maiden's Prayer" at the most interesting part.

Then began an animated drinking of tea in which the Nepman was the center of attention.

For some reason I took offense (so what if he is a Nepman, I'm a person too, aren't I?) and decided to start a conversation with him. And I did it successfully.

"How much do you earn?" I asked the owner of the treasure.

I promptly received two kicks under the table from different directions. On my right foot I felt the poet's

6. A product of the New Economic Policy. Rigid centralized control of all industry was abandoned and a new system was introduced whereby industries were grouped into trusts which were permitted to operate the industrial concerns entrusted to them as individual firms.

boot (a rounded, worn-down heel) and on my left foot the hostess' shoe (a sharp French heel).

But the tycoon didn't take offense. Quite the contrary, he was flattered by my question for some reason.

He rested his eyes on me for a second, from which I could only discern that they were like two counterfeit gold coins made in Odessa.

"Hm-m... how shall I put it?... Oh... it's a trifle. Two, three billion," he answered, spattering me with rays of light from his finger.

"And how much was your sh—" I began, but cried out in pain.

"...Shave?!" I shouted, beside myself, instead of "shining diamond ring."

"My shave cost twenty mil," the Nepman answered in amazement, and the hostess looked at him as if to say, "Don't pay any attention. He's an idiot."

I was instantly removed from the repertoire. The hostess began to chatter, but thanks to my brilliant initiative, the conversation somehow became bogged down in the money mire.

First of all, the poet threw up his arms and said with a groan, "Twenty mil! Oh, no." He had his last shave in June.

Second, the hostess herself came out with some untoward remark about the volume of business at the trust.

The Nepman understood that he was in the company of financial neophytes and decided to put us in our place.

"A stranger comes to me at the trust," he began, his black eyes flashing, "and says, 'I will take two hundred billion in goods from you. In payment I will give you promissory notes.' 'Permit me to inquire,' I answer, 'you are a private citizen... Uh... what guarantee do I have that your esteemed promissory notes...' 'Ah, please,' he answers. And he pulls out his account book. And how much do you think," asked the Nepman, triumphantly surveying those sitting at the table, "he had in his account?"

"Three hundred billion," the poet shouted (this damned sans-culotte had never held more than fifty mil in his hands).

"Eight hundred billion" said the hostess.

"Nine hundred and forty billion," I squeaked tentatively, withdrawing my feet from under the table.

After a pause for effect the Nepman said, "Thirty-three trillion."

At this point I fainted, and I have no idea what happened next.

Note for foreigners—in the Moscow trusts a trillion is a thousand billion. Thirty-three trillion is written as follows:

33,000,000,000,000.

V

The Man in Tails

The Zimin Opera. *Les Huguenots*. Just like *Les Huguenots* of 1893, *Les Huguenots* of 1903, 1913 and finally, 1923!

I have not seen these Huguenots since 1913. First impression—just dazzling. Two twisted green columns and an infinite number of pale blue thighs in tights. Then the tenor begins to sing in a way that immediately gives you an agonizing desire to go to the buffet and call out, "Citizen server, beer!" (There aren't any *sirs* in Moscow yet.)

The thunderous "Piff, paff" of Marcel bursts in your ears, and in your head is the thought: "Probably it's really wonderful if the recent turbulent years haven't kicked these Huguenots out of this theater which is painted in some kind of frog green color."

But boy was I wrong! In the parterre, the boxes, and circle there is not an inch of room. All eyes are fixed on Marcel's yellow boots. And Marcel, sending furious looks into the parterre, threatens:

> Don't expect help
> It will not c-o-o-me...

Low rumbling bass notes.

The soloists, turned blue by the stage makeup, cut through the thundering clamor of the chorus and brass instruments. The curtain falls. Lights. Immediately there is the desire for sandwiches and a smoke. The first is impossible, because to afford sandwiches you have to make about ten billion a month. The second is possible.

By the cloakrooms is a draft, a curtain of smoke. In the foyer is the shuffling of feet, the buzzing of voices, and the smell of cheap perfume. There is the most unbearable melancholy after the cigarette.

Everything is as it used to be, as it was five hundred years ago. With the exception of the clothes, of course. Disreputable suit jackets and threadbare service jackets.

"Just look at them," I thought as I watched. "This audience is not quite the thing..."

No sooner had I thought this than I saw a man standing by the entrance to the parterre. He was wearing a frock coat! Everything was perfect. The dazzling shirt front, the perfectly pressed trousers, the patent-leather shoes, and finally, the tailcoat itself!

He would not have been out of place in a French comedy. My first thought was: perhaps he is a foreigner? Anything can be expected from them. But he turned out to be one of ours.

Much more interesting than the tailcoat was its owner's face. An expression of depressed concern spoiled the rounded features of the Muscovite's face.

His eyes clearly said, "Yes, indeed, a tailcoat, what of it? No one can say a word to me. There is no decree concerning tailcoats."

And, in fact, no one troubled the man in tails, nor did he arouse any particular curiosity. He stood immovable, like a rock around which swirled the tide of suit and field jackets.

I was so intrigued by this tailcoat that I did not listen to the rest of the opera.

I kept wondering, "What is a tailcoat supposed to mean? Is it a museum piece here in Moscow among the field jackets of 1923, or is the man in the tailcoat some kind of living portent?

"What of it. In six months we'll all be wearing frock coats."

You think that perhaps this is an idle question? Not at all...

VI

Biomechanical Chapter

> *Call me Vandal*
> *I deserve the name*

I admit that I hesitated for a long time before writing these lines. I was afraid. Then I decided to risk it.

After I realized that *Les Huguenots* and *Rigoletto* had ceased to entertain me, I embraced the avant-garde with a vengeance. The reason for this was I. Ehrenburg, who wrote the book *But the Earth Keeps on Turning*,[7] and two long-haired Moscow Futurists who visited me every day for a week and severely criticized me over evening tea for my "bourgeois narrow-mindedness."

It is not very pleasant to be taunted with these words, so I went, curse them! I went to the GITIS Theater to see Meverhold's production of *The Magnanimous Cuckold*.

The point is, I am a working man. I earn every million through sleepless nights and harried days of endless rushing around. My money is what they call hard-earned. For me the theater is enjoyment, relaxation, entertainment, in short anything you want except a means to acquire a superb case of nervous prostration, especially since in Moscow there are dozens of opportunities to acquire one without wasting money on theater tickets.

I am not I. Ehrenburg and I am not a wise theater critic, but judge for yourselves:

In the barren, shabby, and drafty theater there is a hole instead of a stage (and of course there is no trace of a curtain). In the back is a bare brick wall with two gloomy windows.

---

7. From Galileo's statement, "Eppur si muove."

In front of the wall is a structure. By comparison, a Tatlin[8] design can be considered a model of clarity and simplicity. Some sort of cages, inclines, poles, small doors, and wheels. And on the wheels are the inverted letters "c y" and "t e." Stage hands move to and fro as if at home, and for a long time it is impossible to tell whether the action has begun.

When it does begin (you realize this because from somewhere at the side a light flashes on the stage), blue people appear (Actors and actresses are all dressed in blue. Theater critics call these work clothes. I would send them to the factory for just a day or two! Then they would know what work clothes are!)

Scene: A woman, lifting her blue skirt, slips down from an incline on which both men and women are sitting. A woman is cleaning a man's behind with a clothes brush. A woman is riding on a man's shoulders, modestly covering her legs with her work skirt.

"That's biomechanics," my friend explained. Biomechanics!! The feebleness of these blue biomechanics, who formerly learned to utter sickly sweet monologues, is beyond compare. And this, you will note, is only a stone's throw from the Nikitinsky Circus where the clown Lazarenko stuns the audience with his incredible flips!

Despondently and persistently they bang someone in the same place with the revolving door. The mood

8. Soviet painter, graphic artist and stage designer (1885-1953). He denied realistic representation in art and worked in the styles of Cubism, Futurism, and Constructivism. In the 1920's he designed sculptures made of glass, iron, and wood.

in the house is like being in a cemetery at the grave of a beloved wife. The wheels turn and screech.

After the first act the usher said, "Didn't you enjoy it, sir?"

His smile was so impudent that I had a burning desire to bio-punch him in the ear.

"You were born too late," the Futurist said to me.

No, this Meyerhold was born too soon.

"Meyerhold is a genius," howled the Futurist. I don't doubt it. Very possibly. Let him be a genius. I don't care. But it should not be forgotten that geniuses are loners, and I am of the masses. I am of the audience. The theater is for me. I want to go to a theater I can understand.

"Art of the future!!" he flung at me, waving his fists.

But if it's the future's, then please let Meyerhold die and be resurrected in the 21st century. Everyone would benefit from this, most of all he himself. He will be understood. The public will be happy with his wheels, he'll enjoy being a genius, I'll be in my grave, and I won't have nightmares about wooden revolving doors.

The devil take this mechanic stuff. I'm tired.

VII

Yaron

The operetta star Yaron rescued me from my biomechanical melancholy and I dedicate these lines to him with heartfelt gratitude. The very first time he fell to his knees before the Duke of Luxemburg, who tapped him on the shoulder, I understood the meaning of this damned word "biomechanics," and when the operetta flew at a carousel gallop around Yaron as though around a pivot, I understood the meaning of real buffoonery.

Make-up! Gestures! Uproar and clamor in the audience! And you can't not laugh out loud. It's unimaginable.

This is a disinterested advertisement for Yaron: Let me assure you, he has exceptional talent.

VIII

What Smoking Costs

By some mechanism order arises from chaos. Some people belatedly find this out in the newspapers and others from bitter, on-the-spot experience during the creation of this order.

Thus, for example, the Nepman I'm discussing became acquainted with the new order in the corridor of a reserved-seat car at Nikolaev Station.

He was generally a good-humored man and the only thing that set him off was the Bolsheviks. About the Bolsheviks he could not be calm. About gold currency— calm. About salt pork—calm. About the theater—calm.

He frothed at the mouth about the Bolsheviks. I think that if a rabbit were injected with a tiny bit of this saliva, the rabbit would die in an instant. Two grams would be enough to poison Budenny's[9] troops and all their horses.

The Nepman had plenty of saliva because he smoked.

When he climbed into the carriage with his suitcase and looked around, a disdainful smirk distorted his expressive face.

"Hm... just think," he started to say... or to be more exact, squeaked, rather than said, "they act like pigs, act like pigs for four years, and now they have taken it into their heads to clean up! What was the point, one asks, of destroying all this? And you think I believe that this will amount to anything? Don't hold your breath. The Russian people are boors."

And he froths at the mouth over them again!

In anguish and despair he threw his cigarette butt on the floor and stamped on it. And suddenly (the devil knows where he came from—it was as if he came out of the wall) someone appeared with a ticket book in his hands and said, taking the prize for brevity: "Thirty million."

I will not attempt to describe the Nepman's face. I was afraid that he might suffer a stroke.

————

9. A famous leader of the Red Cavalry during the Civil War, later a Marshal.

There's quite a story for you, Comrade Berliners. But you keep saying "bolscheviki," "bolscheviki!" As for me, I like order.

———

I go to the theater. I haven't been for a long time. Everywhere are signs that say, "Smoking Strictly Prohibited." And I think, how remarkable, no one is smoking under these signs. How can this be explained? It can be explained very simply, just like on the train. No sooner did someone with a black beard drag two puffs after reading the sign, than a young man with a pleasant but intransigent face popped up: "Twenty million."

The indignation of the black beard knew no bounds.

It did not want to pay. I waited for an outburst from the young man, who was playing good-humoredly with the tickets. No outburst came, but behind the young man's back without any signal from him (Bolshevik tricks!) a policeman materialized out of thin air. It was just like something out of Hoffmann. The policeman did not utter one word, did not make one gesture. No! He was simply the embodiment of reproach, in a gray greatcoat with a revolver and whistle. The black beard paid with incredible Hoffmannesque speed.

Only then did the guardian angel, who had a small elegant rifle on his shoulder instead of wings, step aside and "a good-natured proletarian smile played on his lips" (this is how young ladies write revolutionary novels).

The case of the black beard had such an effect on my impressionable soul (I suspect I was not alone in this), that now, wherever I go, before reaching for my cigarette case, I anxiously check the walls for any kind of printed trickery. And if there should be a sign saying, "Strictly Forbidden," enticing the Russian to smoke and spit, I will not smoke or spit for anything.

IX

The Golden Age

I do not share the Friedrichstrasse's[10] conviction that Russia has finished herself off; and moreover, as I watch the Moscow kaleidoscope, I have a premonition that "everything will work," and we can still go on living pretty well.

However, I would not go so far as to say that the Golden Age has already arrived. For some reason I feel that it will not arrive until order puts forth definitive roots, the indications of which have already clearly begun in such phenomena as all these no-smoking and no-spitting incidents.

10. i. e., the German government.

GUM[11] with its thousands of lights and smooth-shaven salesmen, the resplendent doormen in the state shops on Petrovka and Kuznetsky, "You must take off your coat" etc., these are the magnificent steps on the stairway to Paradise, but not quite Paradise itself.

For me that paradise will not arrive until sunflower seeds disappear from Moscow. It is very likely that I am abnormal and do not understand the great significance of this purely national product, as peculiar to us as chewing tobacco is to the great American heroes in those fabulous films, but it's quite possible that sunflower seeds are just nasty things that threaten to drown us in their saliva-covered husks.

I fear that this thought of mine will seem absurd and incomprehensible to refined Europeans, or else I would say that from the moment sunflower seeds are banished I will have unshakable faith in the electrification of trains (150 km per hour), universal literacy, and so on, which would undoubtedly mean Paradise.

This fond hope first stirred in my heart after I was almost knocked off my feet on Tverskoi by a swarm of old peasant women and urchins with trays, who were scurrying somewhere with cries of, "Dunka! Get going! He's coming!"

As I had suspected, "he" turned out to be the embodiment in gray, not of reproach but of fury.

Citizens, it is a blessed fury. I welcome it.

11. State department store. Moscow's largest department store, located on Red Square.

They must be banished, the sunflower seeds. They must be banished. Otherwise, we will build an electric express train, Dunkas will spit husks into the engine,and the train will grind to a halt, and everything will go to hell.

X

The Red Baton

There is no more fatal delusion than to imagine the extraordinary, perplexing Moscow of 1923 as all of one color.

It is a spectrum. Its light effects are amazing. The contrasts are monstrous. Dunkas and beggars (oh, my God—Moscow beggars! the New Economic Policy was born in patent-leather ankle boots and immediately that dreadful one was born too, in rags, with a nasal twang, and sat at every street corner, whined in doorways, and hobbled along alleys), the loud swearing of the fossilized cabmen and the noiseless gliding of polished cars, placards with world-famous names... and at a newsstand on Strastnaya Square a vulgar, illiterate old woman sells magazines, temporarily filling in for the absent saleswoman.

I swear she's illiterate.

I personally went to the newsstand. I asked for *Russia*, she gave me *Shipping* (the print was similar!!).

That's not it. The old woman began rushing around inside the newsstand. She gave me another one. That's not it.

"What's the matter with you, are you illiterate?" (I asked this facetiously.)

But down with facetiousness, long live despair. The old woman was *really illiterate*.

———

Moscow is a cauldron: They're boiling new life in it. It is very difficult. You get boiled, too. In the midst of the Dunkas and the illiterates a new, organizational framework is emerging, which penetrates all aspects of daily life.

In despair from the old woman with *Shipping* in her hands, in despair from the bestial cabmen who yell vile obscenities, I dove into Stoleshnikov Alley, and where it crosses Bolshaya Dmitrovskaya Street I saw these very same cabmen. There was apparently some kind of obstacle at the intersection. The row of bearded men on coach boxes was not moving. I was shocked. Why was there no loud swearing? Why did the hot-tempered cabmen not forge ahead?

My God! *That* is the obstacle... But apparently it was the obstacle... The only thing in the policeman's hand was a red baton, and he stood completely motionless with the baton raised.

But the cabmen's faces! They were radiant, like at Easter.

And when the policeman, after letting a streetcar and two cars pass, waved the baton and added with an affection uncharacteristic of constables and Shutzmen,[12] "Your turn," the cabmen drove as tenderly and carefully as if their passengers were the severely wounded rather than perfectly healthy Muscovites.

———

Give us order as a fulcrum, and we will move the earth.

<hr>

12. German for policeman.

Moscow, City of Churches

Moscow is best
To this I can attest

The First Panorama: Naked Times

The first panorama was in thick darkness because I arrived in Moscow at night. It was the end of September, 1921. As long as I live, I will never forget the dazzling streetlight at the Bryansk Station and the two lights on the Dorogomilovsky Bridge, showing the way to my native capital. For, whatever may happen, whatever you may say, Moscow is the Mother, Moscow is my native city. So, the first panorama is a mass of darkness and three streetlights.

Moscow then emerged in daylight through a blurring autumn mist and in the following days in a burning frost. White days and a cloth overcoat. Oh, that miserable cloth. The devil's own sackcloth! I cannot describe how much I froze. Froze and ran. Ran and froze.

Now that everyone is fattened on oil and phosphorous, poets have begun to write that these were heroic times. I can conclusively state that I am no hero. It is not in my nature. I am an ordinary man, born to crawl, and crawling around Moscow I nearly starved to death. No one wanted to feed me. The entire bourgeoisie kept their doors chained and through the crack thrust out fake orders and authorizations. Bundled up in orders as though in bed sheets, they splendidly survived starvation, cold, an invasion of lice, the transport tax, and other such hardships. Their hearts became as hard as the stale French loaves that were sold under the clock at the corner of Sadovaya and Tverskaya Streets.

There was no point in going to heroes. The heroes themselves were destitute and survived on some sort of instructions and yellow groats in which they came upon dainty little stones that were like amethysts.

I happened to fall between the two groups, and quite simply a lottery ticket on which was written "death" lay in front of me. Upon seeing this, I seemed to wake up. I summoned up extraordinary, unprecedented energy. I did not die, despite the blows that rained down on me thick and fast, from both sides. One look at my suit and the bourgeoisie banished me to the proletarian camp. The proletariat tried to evict me from my apartment on the grounds that even if I was not a bona fide member of the bourgeoisie, I at least had bourgeois tendencies. But they did not evict me. And they will not evict me. Let me assure you of that. I adopted defensive measures in both camps. I grew a coat of orders, like a dog grows a coat of hair, and learned to survive on the low-carat, multicolored oatmeal. My body became lean and stringy, my heart like iron, my eyes alert. I was hardened.

Hardened, with authorizations in my pockets, wearing my sackcloth, I walked around Moscow and viewed the panorama. The windows were covered with dust. They were boarded up. Yet, here and there, meat pies were on sale. There was always a sign at each corner saying "Distributor No. ...." For the life of me, to this day I do not know what they were distributing. There was nothing inside these places except a spider's web and a wrinkled old crone in a woollen shawl with a hole in the top. The old crone, I still remember, waved her arms and muttered hoarsely, "It's closed... closed, and there's no one here, comrade, nothin'."

And then she disappeared into some trap door.

————

These may have been heroic times, but they were naked times.

The Second Panorama:
From the Top Down

On a gray April day I climbed to the highest point in the center of Moscow. The highest point was the upper platform atop the flat roof of the former Nirenzee Building, which today is the House of Soviets on Gnezdnikovsky Lane. Moscow lay below, visible to its furthest outskirts. Some smoke or mist lay above the city, but through the haze peered innumerable rooftops, factory smokestacks, and the cupolas of Moscow's churches. The April wind swept the platform, and its emptiness echoed the emptiness in my soul. Nevertheless, it was a warm wind. It seemed to be blowing from below, to be rising warmly from the womb of Moscow. It still did not growl like the wombs of large, lively cities, threatening and joyous, but from below, through the thin veil of mist a sound was rising all the same. It was indistinct and weak, yet all-embracing. From the center to the rings of boulevards, from the rings of boulevards to the furthest outskirts, to the bluish-gray haze covering Moscow's outlying regions.

"Moscow is speaking, it seems," I said uncertainly, leaning over the railing.

"It's NEP," replied my companion, holding onto his hat.

"Quit using that damned word," I said. "It isn't NEP at all, it's life itself. Moscow is coming back to life."

My soul was filled with joy and terror. Moscow was coming back to life, that was clear, but would I be able to live? Oh, times were still hard. Tomorrow was uncertain. Nonetheless, I and the people like me no longer ate groats and saccharin. There was meat for dinner. For the first time in three years I was not "issued" boots, but "bought" them. They were not twice the size of my foot, but just two sizes too large.

Below, the city was entertaining and somewhat frightening. The Nepmen were already riding about in horse-drawn cabs and being boorish all over Moscow. Their faces filled me with terror, and I shuddered at the thought that they were filling up the whole of Moscow, that they had gold ten-ruble coins in their pockets, that they would throw me out of my room, that they were powerful, insolent, malicious, and had hearts of stone.

But after descending from the highest point into the midst of it all, I began to live again. They did not throw me out. And they will not throw me out, let me assure you.

Below, joy awaited me, for there is no NEP without a silver lining. The old crones with holes in their shawls were all kicked out. The spider's web was gone, here and there electric lights were shining in windows, and suspenders were hung like garlands.

It was April, 1922.

The Third Panorama: In Full Swing

On a sultry July evening I returned to the roof of that same nine-story Nirenzee Building. The rings of boulevards were lit with strings of lights and these strings stretched out to the edges of Moscow. The dust did not rise this high, but the sound did. Now it was a distinct sound: Moscow was growling, rumbling from within. The lights appeared to flicker first yellow then white in the ink-blue night. The streetcars grated and jingled below, and the muted sounds of bands rose in rivalry from the boulevard.

On a turret a light flickered. A projector whirred and on a screen appeared the white-columned mansion of a landowner. On the lower platform, surrounding the upper, the white napkins on the tables fluttered in occasional breaths of wind, and waiters in tailcoats scurried about with marvelous dishes. The Nepmen had even gotten to the roof. Below me were four flattened heads with low brows and powerful jaws. Four painted female faces stuck out among the Nepmen's heads, and the table was overflowing with flowers. White, red, and pale blue roses covered the table. Only five spots on the table were not covered with flowers, and bottles filled each of these. On the stage someone in a red shirt, with a girl partner in a peasant dress, was singing ditties:

> *In Moscow, Chicherin has*
> *A sheet music publishing house!*

A cadenza spilled from the piano.

"Bra-vo!" cried the Nepmen, clinking their glasses. "Encore!"

A flattened girl, who from above seemed legless, moved daintily towards the table bearing a goblet filled with flowers.

"Encore," cried a Nepman. He stamped his feet, put his left arm around his lady's waist and bought a flower with his right. For lack of space in the goblets on the table, he stuck it in the lady, in the place where her bodice ended and her yellow body began. The lady tittered, jumped, and gave the Nepman such a scalding look that for a long time he stared with glazed eyes, as if through scales. A waiter appeared out of the asphalt and bowed obsequiously. The Nepman hesitated over the menu for no more than a minute and ordered. The waiter waved a napkin, leaned into a porthole and called out distinctly, "Eight Salades Olivier,[1] two sliced tenderloins with parsnips, two steaks."

The hectic, lively stomping of a horn pipe broke out on the stage. Legs with bell-bottom trousers and patent-leather shoes flashed.

I descended to the lower platform, passed through the glass door, and went down the wide, unending Nirenzee staircase. Tverskaya Street welcomed me with lights, automobile eyes, and the scuffle of feet. A dark wall of people stood by Strastnoi Monastery, cars blinked their turn signals, going around it. Above the

1. A tangy, elaborate chicken salad that takes its name from one of Czar Nicholas II's chefs.

crowd hung a screen. The images swam, quivering, breaking into black dots, becoming blurred, disappearing and bursting out again on the white background. An armored train with open platforms went by, gently swaying. On a platform, moving their arms with lightning speed, bedraggled artillery men with bows on their chests loaded a shell into their cannon. A signal was given, the gun shuddered, and a cloud of smoke flew from it.

On Tverskaya Street the streetcars clanged and the roadway was a contorted heap of granite blocks. Braziers burned. Moscow was under repair night and day.

It was the sultry July of 1922.

The Fourth Panorama: Now

Sometimes, it seems there are two Bolshoi Theaters in Moscow. This is the first one. A sign lights up on it at twilight. Red flags appear in the brackets. There is a lighter spot on the pediment where the eagle was torn down. The green chariot is dark, its outline dissolves in the twilight. Night falls. The public garden empties. Ramrod-stiff figures in sheepskin jackets over greatcoats, wearing helmets and bearing rifles with fixed bayonets are lined up. In the alleys, horsemen in black helmets sit astride their mounts. The windows are lit. There is a congress taking place in the Bolshoi.

The other one is like this: At seven-thirty, the theatrical muse's favorite hour, no shining star, no flags, no long lines of guards are to be seen in the public garden. The grand Bolshoi stands as it has stood for decades. Pale, yellow dots of light shine between the columns. The theater's welcoming lights. Black figures flow towards the columns. In about two hours, inside the semi-dark hall, the tiers will fill with heads. Rows of bright triangles and rhombi from the drawn curtains reflect on the dark background in the boxes. There are waves of light on the felt and the triumph of Radames rolls like a wave in the blare of the brass section and boom of the chorus. During the intermissions the theater glows in a red and gold light and seems just as dressed-up as it used to be.

During the intermission the red and gold hall rustles. In the boxes of the dress circle female heads display newly coiffed hair. Civilians sit with legs crossed and stare, as if hypnotized, at the tips of their patent-leather shoes (I bought a pair of them, too). A lone Nepwoman violates the rules of intermission etiquette. Leaning over the rail of her box in the first balcony, she cups her hands into a mouthpiece and excitedly cries for the whole parterre to hear, "Dora! Come on over here. Mitya and Sonya are here in our box!"

During the day the Bolshoi Theater stands yellow and sullen, shabby and worn. Streetcars skirt the Maly Theater and approach the Bolshoi. Once it begins to get dark Myur and Meriliz displays rows of yellow lights in huge glass windows. On its roof a round sign with the letters, "State Department Store," has appeared. In the evening a light is turned on in the center of the sign. Above the Nezlobinsky Theater two lighted lines flash on and off, "Today bank notes 251." On Stoleshnikov Street a billboard with uneven lettering advises: "Why you should buy shoes only at..." On Strastnaya Square a billboard sits on a roof, its advertisements flash on and off, first multicolored, then dark. On the same square, but on a different corner, a cupola bursts into light, then darkens, bursts into light and darkens, "Advertisement."

There are more and more of these flickering, colored lights on Tverskaya, Myasnitskaya, Arbat and Petrovka Streets. Each passing day sees Moscow more awash with lights. Watch lights burn in the shop windows all night and, for some reason, some are lit *à giorno*. The MPO[2] grocery stores are open until midnight.

Now Moscow sleeps without extinguishing all its luminous eyes at night.

From morning on, honks, rings, and whistles pierce the air and clusters of pedestrians dot the sidewalks. Trucks, lumbering and rumbling with chains on their

2. Moscow Consumers' Society.

tires, creep along the old, crumbly, brown snow. On clear days aeroplanes fly out of Khodynka Airport with a bass drone. The streetcars circle on Lubyanka Street just as they used to, darting out from Myasnitskaya and Bolshaya Lubyanka Streets. Past Fyodorov, the first book printer, under the old crenelated wall, one after another they flock downhill towards the Metropole. The murky windows on the first floor of the Metropole are clean, as if cataracts have been removed from them, and display rows of colorful book covers. At night a globe above the entrance shines like a precious stone. State Cinema II. Opposite, across the public garden, Testov has suddenly come back to life and in the entrance displays a menu: peasant soup. On Okhotny Row the billboards are so huge that they dwarf the shops. But Poroskeva-Pyatnitsa looks on sadly and dully. They say it is going to be demolished. That is a pity. How much this street has seen, this narrow alley between windows displaying carcasses of meat, booths of secondhand booksellers, and the white side of a church.

The chapel, which used to be on the small square where Tverskaya Street joins Okhotny Row and Mokhovaya Street, has already been torn down.

The rows of market stalls on Red Square, which for several years were a remarkable example of hideous desolation, are now full of shops. In the center by the fountain, a crowd of people buzzes and shuffles, trading hard currency. Their pleasant faces are marred only by a hint of uncertainty in their eyes. In my opinion, this is quite understandable. GUM has only three exits. This is not the case at the Ulinsky Gates, where the public garden and openness allow you to see far away... Taverns are appearing in epidemic profusion, a veritable revival. Amid the haze and din on Tsvetnoi Boulevard, the sounds of an "authentic" polka erupt with a clang:

> Come, come, dear angel,
> And dance a polka with me.
> Lis-s-s-ten, lis-s-s-ten, lis-...
> ...the polka's sounds are heavenly.

Cabmen now turn in their coach boxes and begin chatting. They complain about the hard times and the fact that although there are plenty of cabmen, people persist in riding the streetcars. The wind buffets the cinema banners which hang across the street. The fences have disappeared under millions of multicolored posters. They extol the new foreign films and announce "Court case against prostitute Zaborovaya for infecting a Red Army soldier with syphilis," dozens of debates, lectures, and concerts. Sanine[3] is denounced, Kuprin's Yama[4] is denounced, Tolstoy's "Father Sergei" is denounced, Wagner is performed without a conduc-

---

3. A love story by M. P. Artsybashev (1878-1927).

4. A book about prostitution and brothels which caused an enormous sensation upon the publication of the first part in volume three of the *Sbornik Zemlya* (*The Earth Anthology*) in 1909.

tor, "The Earth on Its Hind Legs"[5] is performed with military searchlights and automobiles, concerts are broadcast on the radio, tailors sew strelets[6] field shirts, decorating the sleeves with shining stars and chevrons full of rhombi.[7] The stands are filled with magazines and dozens of newspapers...

And so the March sun flashed and melted the snow. The trucks honked even louder in a bass tone, more furious and cheerful. A spur track has already been laid to the Sparrow Hills. There is digging there, lumber is being brought in and wheelbarrows are creaking. They're getting ready a national exhibition ground.

And, sitting at home on the fifth floor, in a room overflowing with secondhand books, I dream of how in the summer I will climb the Sparrow Hills to the spot where Napoleon stood, and I will see how the city's churches gleam on seven hills, how Moscow breathes and glistens. Moscow is the mother.

1923

5. A play by Tretyakov based on *The Night* by Martinet (1923).

6. Literally, shooters. The Musketeers, the first permanent regular regiments of the armed forces in Muscovy. The streltsy regiments were organized in the middle of the 16th century.

7. Chevrons are strips of galloon on the sleeves of the uniforms of soldiers, sergeants, and junior officers in Russian and foreign armies which determine the military rank and years of service. Rhombus is the popular name for a badge of rank of that shape on the uniforms of senior officers in the Soviet Army (until 1943); the more an officer has the higher his rank

Moscow Scenes

I
In the Vanguard

"Well, gentlemen, if you please," the host said courteously and made a regal gesture towards the table. Not requiring a second invitation, we sat down and unfolded the starched, upright napkins.

There were four of us at the table: the host, formerly an attorney; his cousin, also formerly an attorney; another cousin, formerly the widow of an active high-ranking civil servant under the Czar, who subsequently worked in the Sovnarkhoz[1] and was now simply Zinaida Ivanovna; and a guest, myself, formerly... but that does not matter... now a person whose occupation is difficult to specify.

The early April sunlight struck the window and played on the shot glasses.

"Spring is here, thank goodness. We've had enough of the winter," said the host and tenderly grasped the neck of the decanter.

"I'll agree with that!" I exclaimed. I took an anchovy-sprat from the tin, peeled off the skin in a flash, spread creamy butter on a slice of bread cut from a long white loaf and covered it with the sprat's torn

---

1. Council of the National Economy, a government body for the territorial administration of industry and construction in the USSR (1917-32).

body. Then, courteously baring my teeth in Zinaida Ivanovna's direction, I added, "To your health!"

Then we drank.

"Is it still too strong?" the host inquired solicitously.

"Just right," I answered, exhaling sharply.

"It doesn't seem to be strong enough," responded Zinaida Ivanovna.

The men protested in unison, and we drank a second round. The maid brought in a tureen of soup.

After the second shot a divine warmth welled up within me and a feeling of well-being took me in its embraces. I immediately fell in love with our host and his cousin and discovered that Zinaida Ivanovna, despite her thirty-eight years, was not at all bad-looking and that Karl Marx's beard, which was on the wall directly opposite me next to a railway map, was not at all as appallingly huge as everyone assumes. The story of how Karl Marx appeared in the apartment of an attorney who utterly despises him is this.

My host is one of the shrewdest people in Moscow, if not the shrewdest. He was almost the first to perceive that the goings-on were a serious and long-lasting kind of thing, so he dug himself into his apartment, not in the usual amateurish way, but solidly. First of all, he summoned Terenty, and Terenty made a mess of the whole apartment for him, erecting what resembled an earthenware coffin in the dining room. This same Terenty poked huge holes in all the walls, through which he pushed thick, black pipes. After this, the host, enjoying Terenty's work, said, "I don't care if those bandits don't stoke the furnace," and he went to Plyushchikha. From Plyushchikha he brought Zinaida Ivanovna and installed her in the former bedroom, a room on the sunny side. Three days later, his cousin arrived from Minsk. He readily made haste to put his cousin up in the former drawing room (to the right of the entrance hall) and provided him with a small black stove. Then he shoved 540 pounds of flour into the library (just down the corridor), locked the door with a key, hung a carpet over the door, placed an etagere against the carpet, put empty bottles and some old newspapers on the etagere and the library literally disappeared—the devil himself could not have found a way into it. Thus, out of six rooms only three remained. He took up residence in one himself, with a certificate stating that he had a heart defect, and he took down the doors between the two remaining rooms (the living room and study), turning them into a strange double room.

It was not one room because there were two of them, but it was impossible to live in them as if they were two, especially as he had placed a bed in the first (the living room) directly under the statue of a naked woman and next to the piano. Taking Alexandra from the kitchen, he said to her, "They're going to start coming here. So say that you sleep here."

Alexandra smiled conspiratorially and answered, "Very well, sir."

He stuck mandates all over the study door, from which it was evident that he, a legal adviser for some institution, was entitled to "additional space." In the additional space he erected such barricades as two bookshelves, an old bicycle without tires, chairs showing nails, and three cornices, so that even I, who am very familiar with his apartment, on my very first visit after it had been made battle-ready, smashed my knees, face, and arms and ripped my jacket to shreds in front and back.

On the piano he stuck an authorization stating that Zinaida Ivanovna was a music teacher, on the door of her room an authorization stating that she worked in the Sovnarkhoz, and on his cousin's door one stating that he was the secretary. He began answering the door himself after the third ring, by which time Alexandra would be lying on the bed next to the piano.

For three years, people in moth-eaten gray greatcoats and black overcoats, and spinsters with briefcases and wearing canvas raincoats, tore into the apartment like infantry onto barbed wire, and did not achieve a damned thing. Returning to Moscow three years after thoughtlessly leaving, I found everything just as I had left it. The host had just grown a bit thinner and complained that they had completely worn him out.

Back then he had also bought four portraits. He placed Lunacharsky in the living room, in the most prominent place, so that the People's Commissar could definitely be seen from anywhere in the room. He hung the portrait of Marx in the dining room, and above the grand, yellow, plate-glass cupboard in his cousin's room he tacked up L. Trotsky. Trotsky was depicted *en face*, wearing a pince-nez, as is the custom, and with a rather good-humored smile upon his lips. But as soon as the host had punched four tacks through the photograph, it seemed to me that the representative of the Revolutionary Military Council started to frown. Frowning thus he remained. Then the host took Karl Liebknecht[2] out of the package and headed for Zinaida Ivanovna's room. She met him in the doorway and slapping her thighs, over which a striped skirt was tightly stretched, she cried, "I will have n-nothing of that sort! As long as I live, Alexander Palych, there will be no Marats or Dantons in my room!"

"Zin... who said anything about Mara..." the host began, but the energetic woman spun him around and pushed him away. The host pensively turned the color photograph over in his hands and filed it away.

Precisely half-an-hour later came the next attack. After the third ring and a pounding of fists on the colored, ornamental glass of the front door, the host, having discarded his suit coat for a bedraggled field jacket, let in three people. There were two in gray and one in black carrying a reddish-brown briefcase.

2. German socialist revolutionary, founder of the German Communist Party.

"You have rooms here..." the first gray one began and stared around the entrance hall, stunned. The host had deliberately left the lights off and the mirror, coat stand, expensive leather chairs, and deer antlers were lost in the shadows.

"What do you mean, comrades!!" exclaimed the host and threw up his arms. "What rooms are there here?! Believe me, six commissions have been here this week before you. Don't waste your time looking! Not only are there no extra rooms, but I don't have enough space myself. See for yourself"—the host took a piece of paper from his pocket, "I am supposed to have an extra thirty seven feet, but I have thirty-one and a half. Yes, indeed. The question is, where am I supposed to get five and a half feet?"

"Well, we'll see," the second gray one said darkly.

"If you please, comrades!..."

At that very moment A.V. Lunacharsky appeared before us. The three gaped at the People's Commissar of Education.

"Who sleeps here?" asked the first gray, pointing to the bed.

"Comrade Alexandra Ivanovna Epishina."

"Who is she?"

"A maintenance worker," the host answered, smiling sweetly. "She does the laundry."

"But isn't she your servant?" asked the black one, suspiciously.

In response, the host burst into convulsive laughter.

"What a thing to say, comrade! What do you think I am, some kind of bourgeois that I keep a servant! We haven't enough money for food here, and you suggest a servant! Ha-Ha!"

"Here?" the black one asked laconically, pointing to the hole into the study.

"An extra room, thirty-one and a half feet, which I use as an office," fast-talked the host.

The black one immediately stepped into the semi-dark study. A second later a basin fell with a crash and I heard the black one hit his head on the bicycle chain as he fell.

"There you are, comrades," the host said ominously, "I warned you, damned cramped quarters."

The black one extracted himself from the foxhole, his face contorted. His knees were torn to shreds.

"Did you hurt yourself?" the host asked anxiously.

"Ah... oo... m-m... sh... m-m... hah," the black one growled incoherently.

"In there is Comrade Nasturtsyna," said the host leading the way and pointing, "I sleep here"—and the host made an expansive gesture in the direction of Karl Marx. Astonishment spread across all three faces. "And in here is Comrade Shcherbovsky," and he cere-moniously motioned towards L. D. Trotsky.

The three looked at the portrait in horror.

"What is he, a Party member, or what?" asked the second gray one.

"He isn't a Party member," smiled the host sweetly, "but he is a sympathizer. A Communist in spirit. Just like me. We only have executives living here, comrades."

"Executives, sympathizers," mumbled the black one with a frown, gently rubbing his knee, "and what about the plate-glass cupboards? Luxury items?"

"Lux-u-ry!" exclaimed the host reproachfully. "What are you talking about, comrade!! Our last, torn linen is in there. Linen, comrade, is an item of necessity." At this point the host felt in his pocket for the key but suddenly stopped and went pale, for he recalled that just the day before he had placed six silver glass holders among the torn pillow cases.

"Linen, comrades, is necessary for personal hygiene. And our dear leaders," the host pointed to each portrait with both hands, "are constantly showing the proletariat the necessity of personal hygiene. Epidemic diseases... typhus, the plague, cholera, these all arise because we, comrades, do not yet sufficiently realize that our only salvation, comrades, is personal hygiene. Our leader..."

At this point I clearly saw a convulsion pass over Trotsky's face in the photograph and his lips part as though he wanted to speak. The host apparently also saw this, because he was suddenly quiet and quickly changed the subject.

"Here is the lavatory, comrades, here is the tub, but, of course, it isn't working, look, there's a box of rags in it, no time for baths now... here is the kitchen, like an icebox. But there's no time for kitchens now. We prepare meals on the primus stove. Alexandra Ivanovna, what are you doing in the kitchen? There's a letter for you in your room. There, comrades, that's it! I am considering asking for another room. That every day someone tears their knees, it's too much of a nuisance, don't you think. Who should I see about getting another room in this house? For my office?"

"Let's go, Stepan," said the first gray one, waving his hand hopelessly, and all three headed for the entrance hall, stamping their boots. When the steps had faded down the stairs, the host collapsed into a chair.

"There, did you see that?" he shouted. "And that happens every goddamned day! I swear to you, they will be the death of me."

"Well, you know," I answered, "I'm not sure who will be the death of whom!"

"Ha, Ha!" chortled the host and burst out merrily, "Alexandra, put the samovar on..."

That is the story of the portraits, Marx in particular. But let me return to my story.

...After the soup, we ate beef stroganoff, drank glasses of white "Ai-Danil" with the winery's name on the label, and Alexandra brought coffee. Then from the study burst the brittle ring of the telephone.

"Margarita Mikhailna, probably," the host said with a pleasant smile and hurried into the study.

"Yes... yes..." could be heard from the study, but three seconds later there followed a shriek.

"What?!"

The receiver began a muffled croaking, and again a shriek, "Vladimir Ivanovich! But I asked! They're all employed! How can that be?"

"A-ah!" groaned Zinaida Ivanovna, "they haven't taxed him, have they?!"

The receiver was slammed down with all his might and the host appeared in the doorway.

"Have they taxed you?" she cried.

"Congratulations," the host answered furiously, "they taxed you, my dear."

"What?!" Her face erupted in blotches. "They have no right! I said that at the time I was employed!"

"You said, you said," mimicked the host, "you shouldn't have said anything, but looked for yourself at what that scoundrel of a housing superintendent was writing on his list! And it's all because of you!" he turned to his cousin, "I did keep asking you to go and take care of it. And now, if you please, he's tagged all three of us!"

"You're an id-iot!" answered his cousin, turning crimson. "What do I have to do with it? I told that scum twice to mark us as employed! You're the one to blame! He's your friend. You should have asked him yourself!"

"He's a bastard, not a friend!" thundered the host. "He only calls himself a friend! Miserable coward! He only cares about shirking responsibility!"

"How much?" cried Zinaida Ivanovna.

"Five!"

"But why only me?" she asked.

"Don't worry!" the host answered sarcastically. "Our turn will come. They evidently haven't gotten down to our names yet. The thing is, if you are being fined five, how much will they wallop me with?! Well, there's no point in sitting around here. Get ready, go to the district inspector and explain that it's a mistake. I'll go with you. Look alive, look alive!"

Zinaida Ivanovna fled from the room.

"What is this!" the host shrieked angrily. "They don't give you any peace, they don't give you an inch. If they don't come pounding on the door, they're calling on the telephone! We've only just managed to get the confiscation committees off our backs, now it's a tax. How long is this going to go on? What else will they think up?!"

He lifted his eyes to Karl Marx, but the latter sat motionless and mute. From the expression on his face it seemed as though he wanted to say, "It doesn't concern me!"

The edge of his beard was gilded by the April sunshine.

1923

Benefit Performance for Lord Curzon[1]

From Our Moscow Correspondent

At precisely 6:00 a.m. the train ran under the cupola of the Bryansk Station. Moscow. Home again. After the absurd provinces—without newspapers, without books, with wild rumors— Moscow is an immense city, a unique city, civilization, and it is the only place to live.

There they are, the cabmen. They wanted an exorbitant eighty million to go to Sadovaya Street. A deal was struck for fifty kopecks. We set off. Moscow. Moscow. The streetcars were already emerging from the depots. People were already hurrying somewhere. Anything new here in the last month? The cabman turned, sat sideways, and carried on an obscure, ambiguous conversation. On the one hand, he liked the government, but on the other, tires were one-and-a-half billion! He liked May Day, but the anti-religious propaganda "was not appropriate." Just why was not

1. British Foreign Minister (1919-24). He did not agree with Lloyd George's attempts to open commercial relations with the Russian cooperatives and was against all overtures of friendship towards the Soviet Union. He composed a memorandum from the British government which was delivered to the Soviet government on May 8, 1923. The British demanded that the Soviets recall their diplomatic representatives from Iran and Afghanistan and apologize for their allegedly improper actions against the British Empire. The memorandum was presented in the form of an ultimatum wherein the British threatened to cancel the British-Soviet trade agreement of 1921 if the Soviets did not fulfill the demands fully and unconditionally within ten days.

clear. His expression indicated that there was some news, but it was impossible to discover what it was.

A heavenly spring rain fell. I took cover under the leather top of the cab, and the cabman, flicking his whip, continued to rattle on about this and that, calling trillions "quadrillions," and blathering some kind of nonsense about Patriarch Tikhon,[2] from which it was only clear that he, the cabman, was confusing Tseplyak, Tikhon, and the Archbishop of Canterbury.

Home at last! I am never going to leave Moscow again. At 10:00 a.m. I opened *Izvestiya*, but I hadn't been able to get my hands on it for a whole month. On the very first page was "The Murder of Vorovsky!"[3]

So this was it. That something in the cabman's face. Moscow knew of this yesterday. It will be impossible to sleep during the day. I must go out into the streets and see what is going on. But it was not only Vorovsky. Curzon. Curzon. Ultimatum. Gunboats. Minesweepers. Let's protest, comrades!! Momentous events! Moscow was attuned to them. That explained the feeling of electricity in the air!

2. Metropolitan Tikhon of Moscow was proclaimed Patriarch at the All-Russian Church Council of August, 1917. He anathematized the Bolsheviks and condemned the peace of Brest-Litovsk. He was placed under house arrest for proclaiming, "Where is freedom of speech and of the press? Where is freedom of religion?" He was arrested in 1922 for withholding sacred vessels which were requisitioned during the famine of 1921. He was defrocked in 1923.

3. A Soviet Party and government official, literary critic, and writer. He was a passionate propagandist of Marxism. In 1921 he was named the general secretary of the Soviet delegation at the Geneva and Lausanne international conferences. He was killed in Lausanne by White Russians on May 10, 1923.

But despite this, sleep overwhelmed me. I slept until two o'clock. But at 2:00 p.m. I awoke and began to listen. Why, of course, from the direction of Tverskaya Street, a band. There it was again. Another one. On the march, apparently.

At two o'clock it was already impossible to cross Tverskaya Street. As far as the eye could see, an unending human tide surged slowly with a forest of placards and flags waving above it. A mass of old familiar ones, from October and May, but among them glimpses of new ones, manufactured with amazing speed, bearing militant slogans. A black mourning placard floated by, "The murder of Vorovsky—a fatal hour for the European bourgeoisie." Then a red one, "Do not play with fire, Mr. Curzon." "We're keeping our powder dry."

The tide swelled and swelled, making it difficult to push forward along the edge of the sidewalk. The shops were closed, iron gates drawn across their doors. Hundreds of heads looked out from balconies and window sills. I wanted to turn down a side street in order to reach Strastnaya Square by a roundabout route, but on Mamontovsky Street horse carts, two cars, and cabs had become hopelessly entangled. I decided to roll with the flow. A chariot on a flat-bed truck floated above the crowd. Lord Curzon, wearing a top hat and baggy frock coat, with a painted crimson face, rode standing. In his hands he held chains of rope thrown around the necks of Eastern peoples in multicolored, oriental robes, and he was driving them with a whip. A shrill whistle broke from the crowd. Members of the Komsomol sang in unison:

> *Beware, Curzon, write what you choose:*
> *The paper may accept it, but we refuse!*

On Strastnaya Square an opposing tide surged towards the first Red Army soldiers who marched, unarmed, in rows. The Komsomol members hailed them, drawing out the words:

> *Glo-ry to the Red Ar-my!!*

A policeman somehow managed to stem the tide for a few seconds and allowed two cars and a cabriolet to pass along the boulevard. Then he hoarsely shouted at the horse carts, "Take the detour!"

The wave broke out into Tverskaya Street and flowed on. A speculator I know bobbed up from a side street and paused for a look. Noting a banner, he gave a meaningful "H'm" and said, "There's something about this I don't like... But it's probably because I have a hernia."

The crowd swept him around the corner and he disappeared.

At the Soviet, the windows were open, the balcony was packed. In the tide, brass instruments played "The Internationale," Curzon, swaying, rode above the heads. From the balcony, people shouted in English and Russian, "Down with Curzon!"

Across the way, on a little balcony under the obelisk of freedom, Mayakovsky, his awesome square mouth opened wide, bellowed out over the crowd in a ringing bass:

> ... *British lion!*[4]
> *Left! Left*

"Left! Left!" the crowd rejoined. Another tide surged out from Stoleshnikov and turned towards the obelisk. The crowd shouted for Mayakovsky. He again appeared on the little balcony and thundered, "Lord Curzon, who the hell? That name, comrades, doesn't ring a bell!"

And he began to explain, "Behind the mask of a polite lord lurk the snarling fangs of a wolf!!... When the Baku Communists were killed..."

Again the brass instruments at the Soviet began to blare. High-pitched female voices were singing, "Arise, you wretched of the earth."

Mayakovsky continued to fling out words as heavy as cobblestones, the base of the monument boiled like an ant hill, and a voice from the balcony cut through the noise, "We want Curzon's resignation!!"

Endless rows stretched all the way across Okhotny Row, and Teatralnaya Square was obviously packed with people. At Iverskaya the candle flames quivered

4. An improvised version of Mayakovsky's poem, "Left March" (1918).

unsteadily and four old women clung to the icon with labored sighs. The rows swirled turbulently past Iverskaya through both arches of the Voznesensky Gates. Brass trumpets played marches. Here, Curzon was being carried on bayonets, and a worker ran along behind striking him on the head with a shovel. The head, in a crumpled top hat, dangled helplessly from side to side. Behind Curzon, a gentleman rode out through the archway with a placard on his chest, "Diplomatic Note," next, a giant cardboard fist making an obscene gesture and bearing the words, "This is our answer."

I was able to slip along Nikolskaya Street, but on Tretyakovsky the tide again swelled up to meet me. Here, Curzon swung from a rope on a pole. His head was being bashed on the pavement. Along Teatralny Passage gallows bearing wooden skeletons and inscriptions rolled on the human waves: "Here are the fruits of Curzon's politics." At the turn onto Neglinny Street, polished cars were mired in the thick mass of people, and Teatralnaya Square was a solid sea. I have never seen anything like it in Moscow before, not even during the days of October. For a few minutes I managed to bob among the rows and the boiling whirlpools, then I succeeded in crossing the lines of Young Pioneers with flags, then the gray wall of Red Army soldiers, and reached a jammed sidewalk at the Central Baths. Neglinny was clear. Streetcars of every number, routes disrupted, hurried along Neglinny. The streets were clear as far as Kuznetsky Street, but there red dots flashed again and the rows surged. Streetcars ran one behind the other along Rakhmanovsky Lane to Petrovka Street and from there to the encircling boulevard. There were crowds again at Strastnaya Square. A truck with a cage rode out. In the cage sat Pilsudski,[5] Curzon, and Mussolini. On the truck, a small boy blew into a huge cardboard trumpet. The crowds along the sidewalk craned their necks. Above Moscow a yellow hot-air balloon slowly floated towards the east. On its side, part of a familiar slogan could be plainly seen, "... of the world, uni..."

From the basket the balloonists threw out leaflets. Fluttering and appearing black against the pale blue background, they quietly fell on Moscow.

1923

---

5. An ex-socialist who was the chief architect of Poland's independence in the 20th century, and became Poland's first head of state. He had a hatred for Russia, which had treated the Russian Poles with unusual harshness after the abortive Polish revolt of 1863. He became the leader of the Polish Socialist Party in Russian Poland, and in 1905 he organized a "military organization" to commit acts of terrorism against the Russian government.

Travel Notes

Express No. 7: Moscow-Odessa

Departure

The new Bryansk Station is grandiose and clean. To someone who has not traveled anywhere in two years, everything in it seems extraordinary. A tremendous amount of open space, polished floors, porters, and ticket counters by which there are no exhausted, irate people striving to get somewhere with groans and curses. No accursed, sticky, offensive swearing; no dreadful, gray bags; no trampled children, no darting, furtive people who live off stealing suitcases and bundles in the hellish turmoil. In short, the station was simply indescribable. There are not very many pickpockets and the ones there are are all dressed in European style. The porters, it was true, still have an enigmatic look, but now with a certain touch of melancholy. Now you can even buy a ticket a day in advance at the Metropol (there are only five or six people in line) or order one by telephone. And they will send it to your house.

The only time I felt anxious was when, at the platform entrance, I noticed about thirty men and women with kettles, sitting on their suitcases. Suitcases, kettles, and children curved in a line into the main hall. Seeing this line, seeing the tension and sullen concentration with which the people on the suitcases looked at the doors and at each other, my blood ran cold and I turned pale.

My God! Might all this cleanliness, spaciousness, and tranquility be an illusion?! My God! The doors might be flung open, children might howl, glass might fly, a wallet might be "pinched"... A nightmare! Boarding! A nightmare.

Someone walking by wearing a railway cap reassured me: "Don't worry, citizen. They act that way out of stupidity. Nothing like that will happen. The seats are numbered. Go take a walk and in five minutes come back and take a seat on the train."

My heart immediately filled with joy and I went to look around the station.

10:20, to the minute, a red cap could be glimpsed alongside the train, the steam engine whistled hoarsely in front, the huge glass cupola disappeared and outside the windows smokestacks, coaches, and the late April snow scurried past.

On the Road

It's incredible! The station pales in comparison. Compartments for two. Obviously new covers on the seats, curtains at the windows. The conductor came, took my ticket and seat assignment and gave me a receipt. There was a knock on the door. An extraordinarily polite man in a double-breasted leather jacket inquired, "Will you be having breakfast?"

"Oh yes! I will have breakfast!"

There were no protective accordions between the coaches. I went from one coach to the next, over the platforms which rocked with the train's motion, to the next to the last car, the dining car. Enormous windows, the floor completely carpeted, white tablecloths. The steam heating is on, and as soon as you walk in you are overcome with a feeling of lassitude.

A layered, bluish haze settles above the tables, and thickets rush past in the wide windows, followed by fields with white patches of snow, bare branches, groves, and again fields.

And home again to my compartment, through the "hard," formerly third-class, coaches. In the compartment is the same feeling of lassitude, warm air blows from the pipe below the window. The conductor has turned on the heat.

In the evening, after my second trip to the dining car, it begins to get dark. There seems to be less snow in the fields. It already seems to be warmer here. The lamp filaments in the compartment glow, voices sound in the corridor. The words "bank note" and "atheist" can be heard. The gaily colored pages of magazines flash by and the conductor frequently comes in with a whisk broom and throws out cigarette butts. Gentlemen in elegant coats, shoes with pointed toes, and gloves are heading for the dining car. Stations fly past in the twilight. The train stops for a short time, a few minutes. And again the coaches rock, the heat from the pipes intensifies.

At night the first-class coach quiets, people undress in their compartments, the soporific mumbling about bank notes, hard currency, and calculations dies away, and in the heat and sleep hundreds of miles go by, Bryansk, Konotop, Bakhmach.

In the morning it is clear: there is no snow here, it's warm here.

In Nezhin, a young boy with a secretive and agitated face scrambles out from under the train. He has two jugs of pickles under his arms.

"Fifteen mil," squeaks the boy.

"Bring them here!" passengers call gaily, waving their money. But something terrible is happening to the boy. His face contorts and he vanishes into thin air.

"A lunatic!" the puzzled Muscovites say. Next, an old crone scrambles out, but she too disappears in spasms.

The mystery is immediately explained. A ramrod-stiff guard in an ankle-length cavalry greatcoat walks by the coach and irritably mutters, "These damned old crones!"

Then he turns to the passengers, "Citizens! Do not break the law. Do not buy anything from beside the train. There is a shop over there!"

The passengers rush off in pursuit of Nezhin pickles and buy them by legal and illegal means.

About one o'clock, two hours late, the Dnieper appears from behind the Darnitsky Woods. The train runs onto a railway bridge that has been patched up after explosions. It stretches out high above turbid waves, and on the other bank, unfolding in the verdure of the hills, is the most beautiful city in Russia, Kiev.

Rusted tracks run below the embankments. The passenger and freight trains, battered by war, begin to stretch endlessly. Dim, obliterated lettering on a steam engine "Proletar..." flashes by.

A building runs past and on it is a sign in Ukrainian "Kyiv II."

1923

The Komarov Case

Since the beginning of 1922 people had been disappearing in Moscow. For some reason, this happened most frequently to Muscovite horse traders and peasants from villages near Moscow who came to buy horses. Apparently, the person did not buy a horse and then would disappear.

At the same time, strange and unpleasant discoveries were turning up at night. In the empty lots of Zamoskvorechie, in ruined houses and in abandoned, unfinished bath houses on Shabolovka Street, stinking, gray sacks showed up. They contained naked male corpses.

After several of these discoveries, acute anxiety arose in the Moscow Criminal Investigation Department. The thing was, the sacks with the murdered men all bore the same fingerprints—it was the work of one man. The skulls were crushed with the same blunt instrument, the corpses were identically bound, always a neat and skillful job, with the arms and legs drawn up to the stomach. The binding was done firmly, with care.

The Investigation Department began working intensively on the strange case. However, considerable time passed and more than thirty people found their way into sacks among the piles of Zamoskvorechie bricks.

The Investigation Department worked slowly and painstakingly. The sacks were tied in a way that is normally used to harness horses. Might the murderer be a cabman? Traces of oats were found in the bottom of several sacks. Even more probability that it was a cabman. Twenty-two corpses had been found already, but only seven of them had been identified. The investigators were able to establish that all of them had been in Moscow to buy horses. Without a doubt, it was a cabman.

But there were no other clues. There were absolutely no leads from the moment the person sought to buy a horse to the moment he was found dead. No clues, no conversations, no meetings. In this respect the case was certainly unique.

So, it had to be a cabman. Corpses were found in Zamoskvorechie, then again and again in Zamoskvorechie. The murderer had to be a cabman who lived in Zamoskvorechie.

The Investigation Department's dragnet encompassed stables, tearooms, cabstands, and taverns. They were on the trail of the Zamoskvorechie cabman.

In the meantime, the next corpse was found with a new diaper wrapped around its smashed skull. The net immediately tightened. They looked for a married man who had recently had a child.

Among the thousands of cabmen they finally found him.

Vasily Ivanovich Komarov, a cabman, lived at No. 26 Shabolovka Street. His occupational habits were unusual. He almost never hired himself out, but was frequently at the cabstands. He always had money. And drank a lot.

On the night of May 18, agents from the Criminal Investigation Department arrived at the apartment on Shabolovka Street with a warrant from the local police, supposedly for moonshining. The cabman greeted them with unruffled calm. But when they started to open the door of a closet on the stairway, he leapt from the second floor into the garden and managed to escape, despite the fact the apartment was surrounded.

But they were determined to catch him and the very same night they seized him in Nikolsky, a suburb of Moscow, at the home of a milkwoman friend. They found Komarov at work. He was sitting and writing a statement concerning the murders he had committed on the back of his identification papers. For some reason, he implicated and falsely accused his neighbors in this statement.

During this time investigators were in Moscow on Shabolovka Street examining the next corpse which they had found in the closet. When they opened the closet the body was still warm.

———

During the inquest Moscow buzzed with the phrase, "Komarov the cabman." Women talked of pillowcases full of money and of Komarov feeding his pigs with human innards, etc.

Of course, this was all nonsense.

But the real truth that came to light from the inquest was such that it would have been better if there had been piles of money in pillowcases, or even vile pig feeding, or some sort of brutality or perversion. Something intricate and terrible would certainly have been easier, because then it would have been possible to understand the most terrible thing in this whole case, the man himself—Komarov. (A minor detail—he was not, of course, Komarov, Vasily Ivanovich, but Petrov, Vasily Terentievich. The false surname was no doubt an indication of his black, criminal past... but, I repeat, this is not important.)

I assure the reader I have no wish to write a crime-related feuilleton, but I have been unable to do anything else the whole day because my mind has been obsessed with a desire to understand this Komarov all the same.

Apparently, he had some special matting and let the corpses bleed onto these mats (so as not to stain the sacks or the sleigh); when he had enough money he bought a galvanized washtub for this purpose. He killed neatly and with exceptional economy: always with the same instrument, with one blow to the skull, without noise or haste, during a quiet conversation (the murdered men had indeed been those interested in horses—after offering them his horse at the cab-stand he invited them to his apartment for negotiations), by himself, without any accomplices, after sending his wife and children out.

That is how they kill cattle. Without regret, but also without any hate. He made a profit but not a fabulous one. The buyers had approximately the cost of the horse in their pockets. No great wealth turned up in pillowcases, but he drank and ate on that money and provided for his family. He ran a kind of slaughter-house, if you will.

Other than that, he was an ordinary, nasty person, like millions of others. He beat his wife and children and drank, but on holidays he invited priests to his house where they held services and he offered them wine. On the whole, he was a devout person with a difficult character.

For two weeks, reporters, feuilletonists, and the man in the street flaunted the phrase "human beast." This was a dismal, insipid phrase that did not explain anything. But no matter how much the well-orga-nized, slaughterhouse nature of the killings was brought to light, for me personally, it immediately de-stroyed all these imagined "bestialities" and confirmed another theory: "he is not a beast, but in no way is he a human being."

Komarov cannot be called a human being just as a pocket watch from which the works have been removed cannot be called a watch.

———

The trial confirmed this theory for me. The case presented before the court was that of a person who possessed none of the characteristics of bestiality. Though there may have been some particular features obvious to a psychiatrist, to the undiscerning eye he was an ordinary, elderly man with an unpleasant, but not bestial, face, which showed no signs of degeneracy.

But when this creature began to speak before the court and, in particular, when he began to snicker with a low chuckle, I came to understand, not fully but to a certain degree (I don't know how it was for others), that he was "not a human being."

When his first wife poisoned herself, it—this creature—said, "Well, to hell with her!"

When the creature married for the second time, it could not have cared less about knowing where its wife was from or what sort of person she was.

"Why should I care, we weren't going into business together." (Chuckle.)

"Just like that." (To the question of how he murdered. Chuckle.)

"How the hell should I know." (This idiotic saying in answer to many questions. Chuckle.)

"Didn't you feed your suckling pigs with human flesh?"

"No, (hee, hee)... if I had fed them that, I would have had a lot more suckling pigs... (hee, hee)."

This was just the beginning. Everything was this devil-may-care, idiotic, "How the hell should I know" accompanied by snickering. Apparently, he did not see those around him as people. There were either "freaks" or "dummies." He held them in contempt. What is "bestial" about this?! If he had hated with bestiality and killed with fury, it would not have shocked those around him as much as did this incredible disdain. A dog, an animal, would have been tortured by the extraordinary lack of interest Komarov paid his fellow men. His wife was "a Polish, Roman Catholic lady" (hee, hee). "Eats a lot." Neither spite, nor stinginess. "Let this Roman Catholic beggar feed off me." There was no spite, but "I sometimes give her a slap in the face." He beat his children, "to teach them a lesson."

"Why did you murder?"

At once a double explanation. But it was quite understandable. First, for the money. Second, it just happens that "I don't like people." There are certain animals which, if killed, yield a double dividend: both benefit and the knowledge that you are spared the contemplation of one of God's unpleasant creations. A caterpillar, let's say, or a worm... This is what people were for Komarov.

In short, the creature was an illusion in the guise of a cabman. He had a chronic, cold unwilingness to admit that people exist in the world. A disregard for people.

The sinister aura of the "human beast" disappeared. It was nothing so awful. Just exceptionally repulsive.

———

He was to be executed. Was he afraid? No. He is a strong fearless creature.

In my opinion, he even sneered a little at the interviewers, the inquest, and the court. Occasionally he talked some kind of nonsense. But listlessly. With an ironic smile. Are you interested? Allow me. "I would kill a gypsy or a priest..." Why? "Just because..."

But one had the feeling that he had no particular desire to kill a gypsy or a priest, but they had bombarded him with questions about the "freaks" so he said the first thing that came into his head.

The interviewer asked how he felt about what awaited him.

"Eh... it'll happen to us all."

Indifferent, strong, fearless, and very stupid in a human sense. His facetious remarks were senseless, the thoughts were stingy and incongruous. But covering all this stupidity was a magnificent, splendid amalgamation of that particular, putrid arrogance which characterizes many, very many, of the Zamoskvorechie petty bourgeoisie... all of those hicks who move to the big cities.

So much for strength.

One night after a murder, I don't know which one, he drove the bundled exsanguinated body to the Moskva River. A policeman stopped him.

"What are you carrying?"

"What a stupid question," Komarov answered softly. "Have a feel." The policeman really was "stupid." He prodded the sack and let Komarov pass. After that Komarov began driving with his wife.

———

As a result of these excursions, Sofia Komarov appeared in the dock next to her husband.

Her face was also familiar. Such long, doleful faces are frequently seen in Sukharyovka, Domnikova, and Smolensk, the yellow faces of peasant women, wrapped in shawls.

Komarov was taken away when Sofia testified, but in spite of this, she gave the impression that she was withholding something. However, I do not think that she was keeping any particular secrets. During the murders Komarov sent her away with the children. But she may have helped from time to time, tidying up or cleaning after the deed was done. That is woman's work. And there were these excursions.

"Well... the little fool... she's weak," her husband said of her. No doubt the will of her husband weighed like a stone upon this stupid, empty, "Roman Catholic" peasant woman.

———

Sentence?

There is nothing particular to say.

Sentence was first passed on Komarov when the police took him under guard so he could show them where he had buried some of the corpses (some of them were buried near his apartment on Shabolovka Street).

Out of the blue, a crowd gathered. At first there were shouts, the hysterical shrieks of old women. Then the crowd began a low grumbling and pressed against the chain of policemen. They wanted to tear Komarov limb from limb.

It was incredible that the police managed to fend them off and take Komarov away.

The old women in my building also passed sentence on him, "to be boiled alive."

"Beast. Meat grinder. How many orphans has he made by murdering these thirty-five yokels, the son of a bitch."

Three psychiatrists appeared in court.

"Completely normal. Sofia as well."

So...

"Vasily Komarov and his wife Sofia are sentenced to death, the children will be raised by the state."

With all my heart I hope the children are spared the terrible law of heredity.

God forbid that they should take after their dead father and mother.

1923

The City of Kiev

A Historical Digression

In spring white blossoms burst forth in the gardens, the Czar's Garden was clad in green, and the sun set every window ablaze. And the Dnieper! And the sunsets! And the Vydubetsky Monastery on the slopes! A green sea ran down in tiers to the many-hued, caressing Dnieper. Thick ink-blue nights over the water, the electric cross of St. Vladimir hanging up above...

In short, a beautiful city, a happy city. The Mother of Russian cities.

But these were legendary times, times when a young, carefree generation lived in the gardens of the most beautiful city in our country. In their hearts they believed that all of life would pass in white light, quiet and peaceful, sunrises, sunsets, the Dnieper, the Kreshchatik,[1] sunny streets in summer, and in winter snow that was not cold or cruel, but thick and caressing...

...But things turned out quite differently.

The legendary times were cut short and history began thunderously, abruptly. I can point out the exact moment it appeared—it was at 10:00 a.m. on March 2, 1917, when a telegram arrived in Kiev signed with two mysterious words, "Deputy Bublikov."

1. The main shopping street in Kiev.

I swear that not one person in Kiev knew what these mysterious fourteen letters meant, but one thing I do know, history signalled that something was about to begin. It started and then continued for four years. What happened during that time in this renowned city is beyond description. It was as if Wells's atomic bomb[2] had exploded under the graves of Askold and Dir,[3] and for a thousand days flames roared, boiled, and blazed not only in Kiev itself but also in its suburbs and dacha neighborhoods for a radius of ten miles.

When heaven's thunder (for even heavenly tolerance has its limits) kills every last one of the contemporary writers, and when a new, contemporary Lev Tolstoy appears in about fifty years, a wonderful book on the great battles of Kiev will be written. Then the book publishers will make a killing on a grand monument to the years 1917-20.

For the present, one thing can be said: according to its citizens, Kiev changed hands eighteen times. A few self-styled memoir writers counted twelve. I can report that it was exactly fourteen, and I personally lived through ten.

The Greeks were the only ones who did not come to Kiev, and this was an accident since a sensible administration hastily sent them out of Odessa. Their

2. In his book *The World Set Free* published in 1914, H. G. Wells foresaw an extremely powerful "atomic" bomb.

3. Kiev princes of the second half of the ninth century who were killed in 882 by Oleg, a Novgorod prince who captured Kiev.

last word was the Russian word, "Fate."

I sincerely congratulate them on not coming to Kiev. There an even worse fate would have awaited them. There is no doubt that they would have been sent packing. It is enough to recall what happened to the Germans. The Germans, the iron Germans with basins on their heads, arrived in Kiev with Field Marshal Eichhorn and a splendid, tightly drawn-up string of wagons. They left without the field marshal, without the wagons and even without machine guns. The infuriated peasants took everything from them.

The record was set by a famous accountant, Semyon Vasilich Petliura, who was later employed by the Union of Cities. He arrived in Kiev four times, and was thrown out four times. At the very last moment, just before the final curtain, for some reason Polish landowners arrived (scene XIV) with French long-range cannons.

For a month and a half they paraded around Kiev. The people of Kiev, having learned from experience, looked at the fat cannons and crimson piping and said with confidence, "The Bolsheviks will soon be back."

And that is exactly what happened. As the second month waned beneath a cloudless sky the Soviet cavalry, in their usual fashion, rudely showed up where they were not invited and within a few hours the landowners had left the bedeviled city. But at this point I should mention that all those who had previously visited Kiev left in an amicable manner, confining themselves to relatively harmless, six-inch artillery fire on Kiev from positions in Svyatoshinsk. Our Europeanized cousins, however, took it into their heads to flaunt their destructive power and destroyed three bridges across the Dnieper, smashing the Chain Bridge to smithereens.

To this day, instead of a splendid structure rising out of the water, the pride and joy of Kiev, only gray, dismal pilings protrude.

Ah those Poles, those Poles...

The Russian people will give you a hearty thanks.

Take heart, dear citizens of Kiev! At some point the Poles will no longer be angry with us and will build a new bridge for us, even better than the old one. And at their own expense, to boot.

Rest assured. Just be patient.

Status Praesens

To say there is no Pechersk is probably an exaggeration. There is a Pechersk, but there are no houses on most of the streets in Pechersk. There are skeletal ruins, and here and there in the windows is twisted wire, rusted and all tangled. Walking through the empty, echoing, wide streets at twilight, one is overwhelmed by memories. It is as if the shadows are moving, as if there is a rustle from the ground. It seems as though strings of soldiers dart forward and rifle bolts click... and any second a dim, gray figure will rise from the cobblestone road and exclaim huskily, "Halt!"

A string of soldiers seems to flit by and golden shoulder straps gleam dully, a mounted patrol dances in a silent trot wearing short kaftans and hats with crimson tails, here there's a ramrod-stiff lieutenant wearing a monocle, then a dandy Polish officer, then, swearing like hell, the shadows of Russian sailors fly by, their bell-bottom trousers flapping.

Oh, pearl of Kiev! What a troubled place you are!...

But this is only imagination, twilight, memories.

During the day, in the bright sunlight of the glorious parks above the embankments there is serene tranquility. The crowns of the horse chestnut trees are turning green, the lime trees are donning their mantles. Park keepers burn piles of last year's leaves, and the faint smell drifts along the empty paths. Occasionally a figure meanders through Mariinsky Park and stoops to read the inscriptions on the faded ribbons of wreaths. These are the green graves of war. There is a plaque bordered with withered green. On the plaque are mangled pipes, fragments of gauges, a broken propeller. Evidently an unknown pilot fell from above during battle and lies in a grave in Mariinsky Park.

In the gardens there is serene tranquility. In the Czar's Garden there is a luminous silence. The silence is broken only by bird song and the bells of the Kiev municipal streetcar which occasionally drift in from the city.

But there is not a single bench to be seen. Not even a sign of a bench. What's more, the elevated bridge, stretching like an arrow between two slopes of the Czar's Garden, is completely devoid of any wooden parts. The people of Kiev carried off the flooring for firewood down to the very last splinter. Only the iron framework remains and young boys cling to it as they creep along on their hands and knees, risking their precious necks.

The city itself also has sizable holes. Thus, near Czar's Square at the beginning of Kreshchatik only a burned out skeleton remains where a huge, seven-story building used to stand. It is ironic that the building survived the most violent period but could not survive the new economic theories. According to the faithful accounts of the locals, what happened was this. A foodstuffs management department was located in this building. And, as might be expected, there was a head of the department. And, as might be expected, his management reached the point where either he had to go or the office had to be burned down. So, one night a fire broke out in the office. Firemen, a product of the new economic theories, gathered like falcons. The department head came out and hung around among the copper helmets. It was as if he cast a spell on the hoses. Water poured, bad language thundered, ladders were climbed, but nothing came of it, they could not save the office.

But the damned fire, not caring a whit for the new economic theories and not succumbing to witchcraft, spread from the office, climbing higher and higher, and the building burned like straw.

The people of Kiev are a truthful folk and all told the same tale, with one voice. But even if it did not happen this way, the fundamental fact is there for all to see—the building burned down.

But this is of no consequence. Kiev's economy has begun to show signs of vigor. With time, if all goes well and God willing, everything will be rebuilt.

Lights already burn in Kiev apartments, water runs from the faucets, repairs are underway, the streets are clean, and that same municipal streetcar runs along the streets.

The Sights

These are the Kiev signs. What is written on them is beyond comprehension.

Once and for all I will say that I respect all languages and dialects, but, nevertheless, the Kiev signs need to be rewritten.

Indeed it is impossible to strike the last letter from the word "homeopathic" and believe that this will change a pharmacy from Russian into Ukrainian. We need to finally agree on a name for the place where citizens go for a shave and haircut: "haircutters," "coiffeurs," "tonsorial shop," or simply "barber shop."

It seems to me that of the four words—dairyhouse, buttery, creamery, larder—the most suitable would be a fifth, dairy. I could be mistaken about this, but basically I am right in saying that uniformity can be achieved. If it's Ukrainian, then it's Ukrainian. But it should be the same everywhere.

But what, for example, does "S. M. R. ikhel" mean? I thought it was a name. But on a pale blue background the periods after each of the first three letters stand out distinctly. So, they are the first letters of some particular words. Which ones?

When I asked a passing native he answered, "I have to admit I'm not really sure."

"Karasik" is understandable, it means "Tailor Karasik," "nursery school" is understandable because a translation appears for the benefit of the national minorities, "kindergarten," but "smerikhel" is just as indeciperable as "Koutu vserokompama,"[4] and even more staggering than "eating-hole."

Population: Customs and Morals

What a striking difference there is between the people of Kiev and Moscow! Muscovites are go-getters, aggressive, volatile, always on the go, Americanized.

4. Incorrect spelling of acronym for "All-Russian Relief Committee for War Veterans."

The people of Kiev are calm, unhurried, and without a trace of Americanization. But they like people for their American ways. And when someone in an outrageous feminine-looking jacket and atrocious trousers, pulled up to just below the knee, bursts straight from the train into their front hall, they rush to offer him tea and their eyes show a lively interest. The people of Kiev adore stories about Moscow, but I would not advise Muscovites to tell them any. For as soon as your back is turned, they will all call you a liar in return for your telling them the honest truth.

As soon as I opened my mouth and began a dispassionate narrative, my listeners' eyes lit up with such amusement that I immediately took offense and stopped talking. Try to explain to them what a casino is, or the "Hermitage"[5] with its gypsy choruses, or what Moscow taprooms are, where they drink gallons of beer and harmonica bands play songs about Robber Kudeyar "We offer prayers to the Lord...," what traffic is like in Moscow, how Meyerhold stages plays, how there is air service between Moscow and Konigsberg, or what go-getters sit in the trusts, etc.

Kiev is now such a peaceful backwater and the tempo of life is so unlike that of Moscow that the people of Kiev do not understand these things.

Kiev quiets down by midnight. In the morning the officials go to work at the All-Russian Relief Committee for War Veterans, the wives tend the children and the sisters-in-law, who by some miracle have not been laid

5. A night club in Moscow.

off, go off with powdered noses to work at ARA, the American Relief Agency.

As the earth revolves around the sun, so Kiev revolves around ARA. The entire population of Kiev is divided into the lucky cocoa drinkers who work at ARA (first-class people), the lucky recipients of trousers and flour from America (second-class people), and the rabble, who are not in any way connected with ARA.

The marriage of ARA's manager (his fifth) is the main topic of conversation. The ramshackle building which used to be the European Hotel, by which stand the Kiev rickshaws, is a great temple stuffed with salt pork, quinine, and cans marked "Evaporated Milk."

But all of this is coming to an end. ARA is closing down in Kiev, in June the newly-wed manager will be boarding a steamship for his America, and there is much gnashing of teeth among the sisters-in-law. Indeed, no one can say what the future will hold. The new economic theories are slowly seeping into this peaceful backwater, into all its nooks and crannies, the building manager is threatening repair of the heating system and rushes about with some piece of paper on which is written "estimate calculated in gold."

But how can the people of Kiev calculate in gold! They are much poorer than the Muscovites. And, after being laid off, where can a young Kiev lady turn? The market place is small and there are not enough relief committees for everyone.

Asceticism

The New Economic Policy is reaching every outlying district in the country, and it's long overdue. Kiev is now like Moscow was at the end of 1921. It has not yet left the period of asceticism. For instance, cabarets are still banned. In Kiev the shops are open (with only rubbish for sale, by the way), but the "Hermitages" are not glaringly conspicuous and people do not play lotto at every street corner or gad about on pneumatic tires until dawn, getting drunk on "Abrau-Dyurso" champagne.

Rumors

But the people of Kiev compensate for this with rumors. It must be said that there are a great number of old babushkas and elderly ladies in Kiev left with nothing to do. Here more than anywhere else, the turbulent war years destroyed families. Sons, husbands, and nephews either were missing in action, had died of typhus, turned up in a foreign country from which they could not return, or were "laid off due to a cutback in staff." The old babushkas do not get any relief committees, and there are no pensions to feed them because they are not the kind of organization from which one can expect money. In fact, things are intolerable for the old babushkas, and they exist in a strange state. To them it seems that everything is a dream. In this dream-like state they find another dream, a longed-for, different reality. Visions come to life in their heads...

It must be conceded, however, that the people of Kiev do not read newspapers, because of the firm belief that they contain "deceit." But since it is inconceivable for man to live on this earth without information, they manage to obtain news from the Jewish bazaar, where the old babushkas are forced to sell candelabras.

Due to the people of Kiev's isolation from Moscow, their pernicious proximity to the places where all sorts of Tyutyuniks[6] originated and, finally, the belief in the fragility of all earthly things that appeared in 1919, they see nothing improbable in the news items dispatched from the Jewish bazaar.

To wit: the Archbishop of Canterbury was in Kiev incognito to observe what the Bolsheviks are up to (I am not joking). The Pope in Rome declared that "if this does not stop," he would become a hermit. The letters of the former empress were actually written by Demian Bedny[7]...

In the end I became so sick and tired of it that I stopped trying to prove them wrong.

---

6. A Ukrainian ataman who spoke of "our age-old enemies, the Great Russians, and their agents, the Jews."

7. Pseudonym of Yefim Alexeevich Pridvorov (1883-1945), Soviet poet and public figure, one of the originators of socialist realism in poetry.

Three Churches

These are an even greater attraction than the signs. Three churches are too many for Kiev. The Old, the Living[8] and the Autocephalous or Ukrainian.

The representatives of the second of these were dubbed "living priests" by the witty people of Kiev.

I have not heard a more apt nickname in my whole life. It describes the aforementioned representatives to a tee, not only their affiliation but also their character.

In liveliness and ingenuity they yield to only one organization, the Ukrainian priesthood.

They are the complete opposite of the representatives of the Old church, who not only do not show any liveliness, but on the contrary, are sluggish, discomfited and extremely gloomy.

The situation is this. The Old church despises the Living and the Autocephalous, the Living Church despises the Old and the Autocephalous, and the Autocephalous church despises the Old and the Living.

How the good work of all three churches, the hearts of whose priests are fed with evil, will end, I can say with the greatest of confidence: with believers defecting en masse from all three churches and plunging into the abyss of starkest atheism. And the only ones to blame will be the priests themselves, who will have

8. One of the basic groups seeking renewal within the Russian Orthodox Church after the 1917 Revolution. Its members sought to adapt it to changed political conditions; they were loyal to the Soviet government. They were considered collaborators by those loyal to Tikhon.

thoroughly discredited not only themselves but also the very idea of faith.

In the beautiful old Sophia Cathedral, which is filled with gloomy frescos, children's treble voices are tenderly raised in supplication in Ukrainian. From the royal gates[9] emerges a young man who is completely shaven and wears a miter. I will not mention how the glittering miter looked juxtaposed to the whitish face and lively, shifty eyes, so that the followers of the auto-cephalous church will not be upset or take it into their heads to be angry with me (I should mention that I am not writing any of this to be amusing, but to express my bitter disappointment).

Next door in a small church, the ceiling of which is dismally festooned with ancient cobwebs, the old priests are holding services in Old Church Slavonic. The Living priests have also selected a place where they hold services in Russian. They pray for the Republic. The old priests are supposed to pray for Patriarch Tikhon, but this is not allowed under any circumstances and it is thought that they are not so much praying as quietly anathematizing. Finally, what the autocephalous priests pray for, I do not know. But I have a suspicion. And if I am right, I can advise them not to waste their breath. Prayers do not travel that far. The accountant[10] will never return to Kiev.

As a result, the minds of the old babushkas at the Kiev Jewish bazaar have become totally confused. The

9. The central door in the iconostasis in Eastern Orthodox churches.
10. Refers to Petliura.

representatives of the old church have begun holding theology courses; those attending are these same old babushkas (they have nothing better to do). The message of the lectures is simple: Satan is to blame for the whole threefold mess.

The idea is harmless and the courses are ignored, as one would ignore any organization that can harm only its members.

I personally encountered the first unpleasantness arising from these courses. After hearing a number of my remarks about the churches, a kind old babushka who has known me since childhood was horrified, brought me a thick book containing an interpretation of Old Testament prophecies and ordered me to read it without fail.

"Read it," she said, "and you'll see that the Antichrist will come in 1923. His reign has already begun."

I read the book and my patience was exhausted. Using some of the knowledge I had, I proved to the old babushka that first of all, the Antichrist would not be coming in 1923 and, second, the book was obviously written by an ignorant charlatan.

After this, the old babushka went to the course lecturer and tearfully asked that I be shown the error of my ways.

The lecturer read a lecture devoted specifically to me in which it was concluded, just as two times two is four, that I was none other than one of the servants and precursors of the Antichrist, putting me to shame before all my Kiev acquaintances.

After this I swore that I would not meddle in theological affairs, whether they be old, Living or even autocephalous.

Science, Literature and Art

No.

There are no words to describe the black bust of Karl Marx beneath a white arch which has been placed in front of the Duma. I do not know what artist created it, but it is intolerable.

It should not be assumed that the image of the famous German scientist can be sculpted by anyone who feels like it.

My three-year old niece, pointing to the monument, said tenderly, "Uncle Karl. Bwack."

Finale

A beautiful city, a happy city. Above the spreading Dnieper, covered with the verdure of horse chestnut trees, and with flecks of sunlight.

After the terrible years of thunder there is now a great weariness. Peace.

But I sense the trembling of a new life. It will be rebuilt, its streets will again bustle and, above the river that Gogol loved, a regal city will once more take shape. Let the memory of Petliura be gone.

1923